PRAISE FOR
The Soul in the Computer

"How does a 'radical, feminist, non-technical female' get to be an exemplary change agent and thought leader at the venerable Hewlett-Packard? After reading Barbara Waugh's eye-opening and terrific book, you'll know why and how."

—Warren Bennis, Distinguished Professor of
Business Administration, USC, and author of
Managing the Dream and *Organizing Genius*

"The Soul in the Computer is the autobiography of an ideavirus. Avoiding the orthodox prose of many business books and how-to manuals, Waugh shoots straight for the vital arteries with entertaining and fast-moving insights. As a veteran change agent in both the civic and corporate worlds, I found this narrative infused with unadorned common sense and practical relevance. For fresh insights presented in a fresh way, a must read."

—Richard Pascale, author of *Surfing the Edge of
Chaos: The Laws of Nature and the New Laws
of Business*

"Bringing change, imagination, and spirit to every task is an art—and Barbara Waugh captures it beautifully in this story. you'll want to read every page, and then you'll want to act."

—Harriet Rubin, author of *The Princessa:
Machiavello for Women* and *Soloing: Realizing
Your Life's Ambition*

"This is a wonderful example of the metaphor of the World Cafe at work—discovering powerful questions, seeding webs of conversation, cross-pollinating ideas, amplifying what's working, and encouraging patterns of shared meaning to be noticed at increasing levels of scale into a 'new conversation that changes the future.' I loved it!"

—Juanita Brown, president, Whole Systems
Associates, co-creator, The World Café

"Barbara Waugh eloquently articulates why passion is the life-blood that holds most organizations together. The Soul in the Computer shows how a dreamer can make tangible change in one of America's biggest companies. It is required reading for anyone who's ever wanted to integrate both their heart and mind in the business world."

—Chip Conley, author of *The Rebel Rules:*
Daring to Be Yourself in Business

"At once provocative, poignant, painful, and powerful, Barbara Waugh's The Soul in the Computer *is an autobiographical journey of embodied spirituality in corporate America. Filled with story, reflection, hard-nosed decision making, and protocol, this book comes equipped with radical tools available to anyone daring to make a difference; daring to have a vital work place; daring to be employee/employer without selling one's soul and giving up all personal life and concerns."*

—Rev. Cheryl A. Kirk-Duggan, Ph.D., executive
director, The Center for Women and Religion

"This is the story of a practical revolutionary, someone who figured out how to effect positive and significant change in an environment that seemed at first unwelcoming to such changes. The author comes back again and again to simple but very effective tools for change, tools that can be used by 'closet revolutionaries' everywhere to transform corporations and make them partners for social justice. Bravo!"

—Anne Firth Murray, founding president,
The Global Fund for Women

"The Soul in the Computer *is a handbook for those non-conformists who, like Barbara Waugh, see business as a vehicle to uplift the human spirit and alleviate poverty and suffering on our planet. She shows that with a small cadre of banditos at your side, you can make positive social change in any environment.*"

—Dr. Mark S. Albion, author of the New York Times best seller *Making a Life, Making a Living*® (Warner Books, 2000)

"*Barb Waugh epitomizes the saying, 'One person can make a difference.' Reading this book will excite you, inspire you, and—most importantly—ignite your thinking about new ways to lead change and enhance the quality of life for all of humanity. The part in each of us that is hungry for making our unique contribution at work will be fed by Waugh's simple but profound approach to leadership.*"

—Rayona Sharpnack, president, Institute for Women's Leadership

"*A stirring story of a remarkable woman in a remarkable company. The company is remarkable because it, sometimes reluctantly, is willing to absorb new ideas and implement them. The woman is remarkable in her unquenchable determination to listen to the problems around and to find a way to help to solve them—both inside her company and outside in the world.*"

—Robert Saldich, CEO, Raychem (retired)

"The Soul in the Computer *is the jubilant story of someone who's poured her huge heart into work and has made an enormous difference—both at Hewlett-Packard and in the world at large. This is a how-to guide for anyone wanting to create a more meaningful workplace. It is a practical demonstration that every individual can make a difference. I recommend it wholeheartedly!*"

—Chris Turner, author of *All Hat and No Cattle*

"*Loaded with vignettes illustrating potent change tools, this book is must reading for business leaders and change agents who are committed to, or who long for, business and global transformation. It reads like a soulful thriller, and offers renewed hope, creative insights, and pragmatic guidance for our own journeys.*"

—Bill and Marilyn Veltrop, co-founders of PathFinders

"*I want to read the introduction to this book each morning before going to work. It has confirmed my belief in my own work, and has helped me be more courageous and effective at helping our customers do theirs. I know that Waugh is right when she says that companies, and the individuals who make up companies, want to do the right thing—I have the honor of working with these people every day.* The Soul in the Computer *not only inspires, it moves you to action.*"

—Lisa Acree, senior manager, Business for Social Responsibility

"*Corporations are full of people who, when they bring social justice values to bear, can change the world. Barbara Waugh shows, with courage and creativity, how to do it in one progressive corporation.*"

—Dr. Marga Buehrig, former president,
The World Council of Churches

"The Soul in the Computer *is a passionate, brilliant story of instinct and right brain/left brain thinking. But most of all it is a deeply resonant call for our humanity and our technical genius to join in a union for future generations. Barbara Waugh is clairvoyant in her undertaking of where the future needs to be. A must read.*"

—Bill Strickland, executive director,
Manchester Craftsmen's Guild and Bidwell
Training Center, MacArthur Fellow

The
Soul
in the
Computer

The *Soul*  *in the* *Computer*

The Story of a
Corporate Revolutionary

Barbara Waugh
with Margot Silk Forrest

INNER
OCEAN

Library of Congress Cataloging-in-Publication Data

Waugh, Barbara.
    The soul in the computer : the story of a corporate revolution
ary / Barbara Waugh, Margot Silk Forrest ; forewords by Alan
Webber and Joel S. Birnbaum. --Makawao, Hawaii : Inner
Ocean, 2001.
        p. ; cm.
    Includes bibliographical references and index.
    ISBN 1-930722-03-6
    1. Waugh, Barbara. 2. Hewlett Packard Company. 3.
Success in business. 4. Success. I. Forrest, Margot Silk. II.
Title.

HF5386 .W38 2001
650.1--dc21   CIP

Inner Ocean Publishing, Inc.
P.O. Box 1239
Makawao, Maui, HI 96768-1239

Cover design: Bill Greaves
Cover photos: Imagine Bank, Stone
Interior page design and typography: Beth Hansen-Winter
Copy Editor: Barbara Doern Drew

Printed in Canada by Friesens

9 8 7 6 5 4 3 2 1

For my soul sister, Lahe'ena'e Gay (November 7, 1959–March 4, 1999)
who believed in corporate revolutionaries and me and HP,
who was murdered in Colombia, helping the Uw'a build their own schools,
and who goads me daily, hourly, to go bigger, bolder, braver, and faster,
because we are still destroying faster than we are saving or creating.
And for all who have played a part in this story
and for all of us who will take it from here,
in the faith that in our lifetime the corporate sector will step up to partnership
with other sectors in stewardship for the planet,
for the seventh generation.
Let us remember these words:

Until one is committed there is hesitancy,
the chance to draw back
always ineffectiveness.
Concerning all acts of initiative (and creation)
there is one elementary truth,
the ignorance of which kills
countless ideas and splendid plans:
that the moment one definitely commits oneself,
then Providence moves too.
All sorts of things occur to help one
that would otherwise never have occurred.
A whole stream of events issues from the decision,
raising in one's favor all manner
of unforeseen incidents and meetings and material assistance,
which no one could have dreamt would have come their way.
I learned a deep respect for one of Goethe's couplets:
"Whatever you can do or dream you can, begin it.
Boldness has genius, power, and magic in it!"

—W. H. Murray
The Scottish Himalayan Expedition, 1951

CONTENTS

WARNING! LIFE-CHANGING EXPERIENCE, DEAD AHEAD!

By Alan Webber,
Founding editor, *Fast Company* magazine

There are people in the world who, when you meet them, will change your life.

They do it by rearranging your sense of what is possible—opening you up to whole new avenues of opportunity and self-expression. They do it by convincing you that the only limits to your future are those that you unknowingly impose upon yourself. They do it by demonstrating that the biggest risk that you can take is not to take risks.

They do it by expressing the absolute conviction that you have within you dreams and aspirations that you've never acknowledged—and then by matching that absolute conviction with the absolute confidence that your dreams matter, absolutely. They do it by making available tools, tactics, tips, and techniques that work—field-tested devices to let you move beyond inspiration to application.

And they do it by unleashing the power of irresistible, fundamental, and powerful emotions into the all-too-often emotionless world of work. In the process, they tap into a heartfelt belief in the sanctity of the individual, the dignity of work, and the invulnerability of good people working together.

Taken together, they show all of us that it is possible to change the world.

Barbara Waugh will change your life. She is a walking, talking, living, breathing, working, playing affirmation of all things possible—one full-time affirmation of the human spirit in the world of work—and for the world. I know this is true because she changed my life.

I had never met Barbara when *Fast Company* profiled her. All I knew was that other people—people whose lives Barbara had already touched and changed—all assured me that she was an amazing person, a remarkable person, just the kind of person that *Fast Company* should be writing about. (And, these people all told me, the really amazing thing about Barbara is, she doesn't even know how amazing she is! She thinks that she's ordinary—and that makes her even more extraordinary.)

Then, after we wrote about Barbara, we invited her to one of our live events. She spoke to the group and blew everyone away. Then we invited her to the next live event. She spoke to that group and blew everyone away again. And then, at one of these events, Barbara and I went for a walk, late one night, and we just started to talk—about our families, about our work, about the jobs we've had, about the fears we have, about the hopes we share.

It wasn't that Barbara is a great talker, and that what she said changed my life—quite the opposite. It was that Barbara is a great listener, and how she listened changed my life. And then, before I knew it, I discovered that I was a part of this magic, mysterious, mystical Barbara Waugh Circle of Friends, and I was getting e-mails and visits and phone calls and messages from the most amazing, disparate, positive, making-stuff-happen group of people on the face of the Earth. From all over the Earth.

There is a simple explanation for all of this, and it's contained in this book. I'm not even sure that Barbara knows it, but it amounts to her own personal recipe for making the world a better place *for everyone*. First come aspirations—it all starts with the dream. Now, the way Barbara sees it, it doesn't have to be a "big" dream. Or a fancy dream. It doesn't even have to be your dream—it could be a dream that someone else has and shares with you. (In fact, that could be the best dream of all, because it tends to underline the point that all of our dreams are interconnected, whether we know it or not.) But from the dream, from the aspiration, comes the moving power, the capacity of each of us, and all of us, to make a difference.

Second come the tools. You have to have tools. There's very little point in being a corporate revolutionary if you don't embrace the tools of your trade. After all, the point of the exercise is not to die nobly and romantically for your cause! The point of the exercise is to *live* nobly and romantically for your cause—and to bring about meaningful changes that can improve the lives of as many people as you can possibly touch. That takes practical, useful, experience-tested tools.

Third comes . . . *you*. That's right, you. Think of it this way: You are the lucky recipient of a personal, fun, hand-crafted invitation to the revolution, courtesy of Barbara Waugh! All you have to do is to show up. Oh, and remember to bring along everything you care about, everyone you know, all the places you've ever been, all the books you've ever read, all the ideas you've ever entertained—bring along all of you. Leave nothing behind, because where you're headed—where we're all headed, which is smack into the future—you're going to need it all. It's all relevant, it all counts, it all contributes.

By the way, take a close look at this idea of being a corporate revolutionary. Don't misunderstand the term. Barbara isn't declaring a revolution *on* global corporations, she's declaring a global revolution *through* corporations. The point is not that business is the bad guys. The point is, *we* are business! We all spend too many hours at work, engaged in too many genuinely interesting, exciting, and challenging activities to assume that, somehow or other, "they" are in charge and we're the unwitting dupes of a vast corporate conspiracy that we need to overthrow. To rewrite the famous line from Pogo, "We have met our allies, and it is us!" If we want to make a global revolution, Barbara is telling us, we've got everything we need right here in our own hands—all we have to do is all join in the task and get to work.

Just in case this all sounds too ethereal and you're still wondering what you can possibly get out of this truly remarkable book, let me offer you six principles that are at the heart of Barbara's message—just a small sampling of the truth, wisdom, and gentle prodding from which you'll benefit if you let Barbara into your life.

1. *Work and life are not two different spaces.* You'd better believe it: Work isn't something you put on like a uniform when you get up in the morning and shed in the evening when you get home. Work and life

are two sides of the same coin—and they're both alive in you. Want to have more fun, more satisfaction, more impact in your work life and in the world? Make sure that it's a fundamental part of your *whole* life. Want to feel like your life has a sense of purpose, meaning, and direction? Do work that gives you an emotional high, that ennobles you, and those around you. Hey! Why be schizophrenic when the whole point of the new economy is to be a whole person!

2. *There is no "them" and "us."* (All she is saying is give people a chance.) No question, we live in cynical times. And one simple way to make sure that you're never caught with your guard down is to assume that "they" are on one side, and "we" are on the other. Unless you actually want to get up in the morning convinced that what you're about to go off and do is going to matter. Unless you actually want to extend your personal circle of growth and influence to your work, your community, and your world. Unless you want to stay alive to a sense of possibility, and stay open to learning new things. Then you've got to admit to the possibility that people with whom you don't automatically agree—who don't look like you, or sound like you, or sometimes think like you—can come to appreciate the things that you care about. And vice versa. Once you open yourself up to that possibility, all of a sudden you open yourself up to a whole universe of other possibilities.

3. *Big change comes in small steps.* Welcome to the age of the short attention span and the shrinking time period: nothing, it seems, is more important than instant gratification and grand gestures. Except in the real world, where Barbara lives. And there, change is possible, even inevitable. That is, *if* you are willing to adopt an approach that is pragmatically romantic: We're going to win, Barbara says, but victories come in small steps. Not that they're any less sweet for being small—fact is, small victories can be even sweeter, the kinds of little advances that you can savor and smile about. But remember to take it as it comes. Care deeply, think bigger, dream longer, try softer—and win a little bit at a time.

4. *The single biggest obstacle we all have to overcome is fear.* What is it that keeps us all from doing what we're capable of? We tend to say, reflexively, that it's "them." (See point number two above.) Truth be told, it's us. It's fear of being different. Fear of sticking out. Fear of exposing ourselves to others. The fact is, if you want to make a difference, you have to *be* different. If you want to stand up, you have to be willing to stand out. And if you want to be yourself, you can't check yourself at the door when you show up at work in the morning. So, Barbara says, don't let yourself scare you out of doing what you know you're capable of. There's nobody here for us to be afraid of—except us.

5. *The way it is isn't the way it has to be.* This may be

the most fundamental principle of all. We all enter a world that is the way it is—and we all need to be realistic enough to see things as they are. But there's a difference between being realistic and being re-signed. None of us has to be resigned to accepting things as they are, or confusing things as they are with things as they have to be. And so, says Barbara, remember: *you are the company.* And you are the change you want to create.

6. *Globalization is a fifty-cent word for a common sense notion.* Just how big is the world? And how hard is it to move it? Not very, says Barbara. It's about as big as a neighborhood and about as closely intertwined. Take a look around the corner, she says, or around the continent, or around the globe. We're all in it together, separated only by distance not by purpose, values, or interests. And what does it take to move this world—or even better, to rock it? Trying. Reach-ing out. Making connections. Anyone can do it, Bar-bara says, and all of us must.

Those are six fundamental truths, and I haven't even scratched the surface of Barbara's remarkable book. Just as a bonus, here's a seventh truth: This may be Barbara's life, but it's all of our stories. I don't know anyone who isn't grappling with these elemental questions of work and life and social responsibility: How can we be ourselves and still feel accepted and appreciated in a world that often seems to reward only conformity? How we can make more than just a living—how can we make a difference in the world? How can we tap into the creativity and energy that we know is inside us, when so much of our work seems to be about rote behavior and auto-pilot performance? The new economy offers us all an opportunity to step out of the past and into an invigorating, exhilarating, challenging—and yes, sometimes exasperating and risky—world of economic change and personal growth.

Are you ready to make the leap? If you pick up this book and enter the world according to Barbara Waugh, be warned: Barbara Waugh changes people's lives. Read this book. She changed mine. She'll change yours. And together we'll change the world.

A RARE COMBINATION OF PRAGMATIST AND DREAMER

By Joel S. Birnbaum, Senior Vice President of Research and Development, Director of Hewlett-Packard Labs Emeritus

*b*efore reading this startling work, I thought Barbara Waugh had, at last, run out of ways to surprise me. We have known each other for ten years and during that time she has, on innumerable occasions, produced an insight, a perspective, or a criticism that has caught me completely off guard. These turned out to be right so often, I wondered how she had managed to reach such different conclusions than her colleagues. But as the years went by, I gradually calibrated her radical's approach to corporate life, and began to sense the method behind the madness. Indeed, more than once, I was a co-conspirator.

Now Barbara has written no less than a how-to manual for corporate revolutionaries—businessmen and women who want to do well for their companies but also want to do well for their companies but also want to improve the world through responsible globalization—and once again I find myself in awe that she has had the cleverness to place seemingly disparate activities into a tapestry of tools and processes that can be reused by others. While the examples and challenges recounted here are intensely personal, I view this work as a primer for accomplishing far-reaching cultural change within any organization, local or global. I know from experience that Barbara's form of corporate revolution is far more likely to produce enduring practical results than many of the conventional consulting/management tactics widely in use today. I can see no reason why many of the lessons learned here would not scale to global dimensions.

Seen with some historical perspective, it becomes manifest that there are unifying principles behind the seemingly disparate anecdotes and outcomes documented here. Driving everything is the fundamental belief that most of the time, if people are given the opportunity to do the right thing, they will invest time and energy to do the very best they can. Barbara combines this doctrine, which is at the heart of "the HP Way," with a credo that is based on inclusion, on having people at all levels of an organization participate in the creation of the vision, the definition of goals, the allocation of resources, and the conquering of execution challenges. It is Barbara's passionate belief that people at all socioeconomic levels must be able to participate in the processes and decisions that affect their lives—and who is to say that she is wrong?

Her style is the antithesis of top-down, hierarchical mandates, or of the external-consultant proclamations so common today. Instead, it is a form of organizational jujitsu, where leverage of grassroots beliefs and talents can produce dramatic results, amplified because people from all parts and levels of a group are able to contribute to a goal or vision that they have helped to shape. Her style is also a reminder that it is important that the vision and goals be worthy, and that if they are, noble behavior will be the rule and not the exception.

In this book, Barbara details many of the process improvements and new programs that resulted from application of these ideas in the "World's Best Industrial Research Laboratory" initiative at HP Laboratories. Unquestionably HP Labs is today a more pleasant and efficient place to work than before we started, but improvements in how we work tell only a part of the story. A corporate research organization must, in the end, be judged by what it does: by the quality of the vision implied by the research agenda that it pursues, and by the effectiveness with which it meets the technical challenges it presents.

I think that for HP Labs, the enduring value of the "World's Best" program will derive from the creation of a cultural climate in which it has become acceptable to discuss openly and honestly the strategic priorities that drive annual resource allocation, and from the removal of the barriers for interdisciplinary innovations, as teamwork became the expected norm. Barbara tells in some depth how we created the climate to produce a world-class research agenda; she touches only briefly on a few examples of the results of that effort. The end of the business story will be told through the HP and Agilent annual reports in the years to come as the innovative products resulting from HP Labs technologies come to market and, in some cases, redefine the ways we live and work. However, the more enduring value of the World's Best program may well lie in the evolution of its vision from being best *in* the world to being best *for* the world, and in the adoption by other companies of this humanitarian vision.

Barbara has collected and codified the tools and techniques that are the basic vocabulary for achieving these results. She has stressed that these are gardening tools for cultivating an environment where change can grow, not a set of machine tools for management to hammer things down. It is an essential difference and, properly applied, can produce results that last, results whose outcome is measured not only by the bottom line and by history, but by the satisfaction and well-being of the contributors.

Barbara is that rare combination of an idealistic dreamer and a results-driven pragmatist, and this book presents ample chances to admire her adroitness at turning a problem on its head, converting a liability into an advantage, and persevering patiently to allow the garden to mature. As you join her on her remarkable personal odyssey, you will hear the voice of a unique human being, one who blends sensitivity, personal courage, and creativity, and whose passionate voice urges us all to choose a star and reach for it, but not by ourselves. If we are wise enough to listen, then, like Barbara, we too can have the satisfaction of knowing that we will leave the world a better place than we found it.

WELCOME TO THE GARAGE

In America, the garage is not just a place to protect old cars, old magazines, record albums and toasters that will definitely be repaired someday. It is a laboratory, a skunkworks, a stage, a studio, where dreamers have transformed fantasies into industries that have changed the world. The garage is, in a way, the U.S.'s secret weapon, a partial explanation of why Americans still seem to have an inventive edge.

—Erik Calonius, *Fortune* magazine

*The garage birthed the high-tech culture. The soul of that cul-*ture has been—up until now—the blood, sweat, brains, and tears that human beings poured into the creation of ever faster, ever smaller, ever cheaper, and ever quicker-to-market computers. (This is the "soul" that Tracy Kidder was referring to in his 1981 landmark book on the computer age, *The Soul of a New Machine.*)

But things are changing. Back then, the machine itself was the point of all that self-sacrificing human effort, all that "soul." Now, *what people can do* with the machine is the point. And, more and more, *the good people can do* is the point. We are entering the age of the soul in the computer.

"Soul in the computer" may seem like the quintessential oxymoron, like "responsible globalization" or "airplane food." But as the airlines have learned, it is in resolving these contradictions and moving onto a higher-level playing field that the future and the competitive advantage lie. So now we get Starbucks coffee and Wolfgang Puck dinners in midair, and people actually choose an airline—all other things being more or less equal—for the food.

More and more, computers, like many other products, are becoming commodities. Companies worry how they will differentiate their products from others just like them. At the same time, there's a lot of research to suggest that, other things being more or less equal, people will buy the products they associate with good for the world, sustainability, social responsibility—in short, soul. So it may well be that the future of the computer lies in its link to, foundation in, and application on behalf of soul.

If that is the case, it is corporate revolutionaries who will forge that link, build that foundation, and create those applications. And we are not as scarce on the ground as the stereotype of "corporation" would have us believe. In fact, the cubicles of the corporate world are teeming with revolutionaries. I know because I meet us everywhere. But too many of us remain isolated, never sharing our ideas, our passions, our deep objections to "business as usual."

The goal of this book is to invite us all to come out and play together and to share the tools that have helped me. I have spent seventeen years at Hewlett-Packard as a corporate revolutionary, and while it's brought me my share of frustration, it has also brought me—to my astonishment—a great career and, most importantly, success in raising the bar on corporate citizenship.

I believe the future of the planet depends on the corporate sector stepping up to soul: our share of steward-ship for the planet and life on Earth. We can no longer leave this vital work to the religious, nonprofit and government sectors.

I believe corporations can step up, must step up, and will step up. I believe it because I've experienced, from the inside, what can happen in a good company. I believe it because I know there are many good companies out there, and a lot of people inside them who care—people who are working on orienting our companies toward "doing well by doing good." And I believe it because there are a lot of good people and organizations outside our companies who are insisting on new levels of accountability and citizenship for the corporate sector. It will take all of us.

I started writing this draft of the ongoing book in my life in the wake of the Seattle demonstrations against the World Trade Organization in November 1999. I knew ahead of time they were coming and saw on the evening news the huge crowd of angry protesters outside the locked doors behind which the WTO was meeting. I could understand their anger. I felt it too. The WTO meets in private, keeps no record of its deliberations, allows no appeals, and makes decisions that can override local interests, even the democratic process, by overturning state and national laws.

As the protesters' fists pounded the door, I thought that many of us inside corporations could be on either side of that door—and are, in fact, on both sides of it. Our political selves are on the outside with the demonstrators; our working selves are on the inside with the corporations. But as we integrate our lives, bring the whole person to work, wake up and "get" who each other really is, we can become a critical force in helping to shift the direction of globalization in favor of all the people of the world, including the future generations of our own families.

The metaquestion of this book and of my life right now is this: Are the evils of globalization inevitable? I say no. Together inside our companies, with our friends on the streets, and with the people throughout the world currently suffering from poverty, disease, and the negative effects of globalization, we can develop a world that works for everyone. I am at the very beginning of understanding how this partnership at all levels can unfold. This book and my life are only first steps in that direction.

◆ ◆ ◆

Many folks have asked for this story about my years as a corporate revolutionary at Hewlett-Packard. Some, because they've heard pieces of the story and want the whole thing; others, because they want to hear more on the tools I talk about when I tell my story; and a few, because they still believe that "corporate revolutionary" is an oxymoron: Either you're a revolutionary, outside the evil, money-grubbing corporation, or you're inside and you've sold out.

I hope this book will help change people both inside and outside the corporation at a number of levels. For example, I hope that together we can move beyond the shunning one of my HP colleagues recently experienced at the hands of the "good guys." My friend is an organic and self-sustaining farmer of forty acres in southern Oregon. That's on the family level. On the company level, he is an applications manager for the effort HP has started to help the world's rural poor and is doing a lot of work with coffee growers.

He was at a conference on organic farming recently when the participants started in on corporations, trashing them all, calling them the source of all evil. So my friend stands up and says, "Hey guys, *I'm* one of them." And suddenly no one wants to talk to him. He's a pariah. It hurt, he told me, to be in the middle of incredibly wonderful discussions and suddenly not be welcome at them anymore.

No, the corporations don't have a monopoly on either/ or thinking or the myopia that blinds us all to the possibilities of breakthroughs.

I hope you find that my story and these tools suggest the possibility of a new world, a world beyond either/or, beyond profit/nonprofit: the world of the social entrepreneur. Social entrepreneurs combine the profit objective, business models and processes of the corporate sector with the values, vision, and social goals of the nonprofit sector in order to produce sustainable solutions to the intractable problems of social equity that have plagued the planet since time began.

As Lew Platt, our former CEO, put it, "The best way to do *well* may be to do *good*." As banker Muhammad Yunus, a hero for many in the developing as well as the "developed" world, might put it, "The best way to do *good* may be to do *well*."

I hope my journey helps as you make your way through your world, whether it's corporate, nonprofit, NGO, or home. Please look at the invitation at the end of the book to share your own stories of revolution, and let me know how to make the next edition of these memoirs more useful to you. There is also room back there to join the conversation, to write your comments—questions, thoughts, whatever comes up before you pass the book on. (John Seely Brown, the brilliant chief scientist at Xerox, once said that the most useful book to him is one passed on by a friend, one that includes his friend's questions, ideas and comments.) Pass it on and follow up. Start a conversation that matters, complete with all the doodled ideas and marginal notes that the text inspired in you.

How to Use This Book

When I came to HP in 1984, I brought with me a box full of tools for change that I had accumulated during my years in the civil rights movement, the peace movement, the women's movement, and my time at graduate school in theology, and later in psychology. I added to the toolbox over the years through my readings in religion, business, and psychology, and my experience in the corporation.

As you read these memoirs, you will notice that the names of the tools I use are highlighted in the margin.

They look like this:

Radical Stand	Radical Move	Radical Tool
PUT A STAKE IN THE GROUND	RECRUIT CO-CONSPIRATORS	TURN "ENEMIES" INTO ALLIES

If you want to learn about the tools first, turn to "Tools for Revolutionaries" at the end of the book, then come back and skim the memoir section (chapters 1–7) for more examples on how to use a tool that you think could be helpful to you.

One caveat. The word *tool* usually connotes something that is used to build or fix something, such as a faulty machine. But one of the most important aspects of my work as a corporate revolutionary is the recognition that the organization is *not* a machine, it's a living system. You can't just haul out a wrench and fix an organization, or fetch your entire toolbox and set about re-engineering it.

You have to cultivate an organization, like a garden. So to me, these tools are gardening tools, like a shovel, a rake, a trowel, and a hoe. Tools that honor the mystery and vagaries of life, that work in the service of life.

Bill Hewlett and Dave Packard built machines in a garage. The new Hewlett-Packard builds machines, too, but the organization that builds them is a garden, full of everything from dandelions and chickweed to poppies, fountain grass, ferns, sunflowers, and climbing roses (complete with thorns).

These are the gardening tools I keep in my corner of the HP garage. I use them for working in the HP garden, for tending the wild beauty of a living organization.

1. RADICAL STAND: PUT A STAKE IN THE GROUND
   • Remember Who You Work For
   • Commit
   • Keep the Faith
   • Be the Change You Want to See

2. RADICAL MOVE: RECRUIT CO-CONSPIRATORS
   • Tap the Strength of Your Relationships
   • Start a Conversation—and Listen!
   • Build Your Cadre

3. RADICAL TOOLS: USE THE RIGHT TOOL
 • Scale Up, Scale Down
 • Amplify Positive Deviance
 • Turn "Enemies" into Allies
 • Reframe the Context of What You're Doing
 • Go to a Larger Context
 • Play with Whoever Shows Up
 • Tweak, Don't Toss
 • Hold Up a Mirror

It's Us and Them

The convention of memoirs is very I-centric, but the reality is that every single thing I've done has been in collaboration with somebody just as fired up as I was about it. My story isn't me (or us) vs. them, it's *we*. Doing it together. Always.

Often, it wasn't the alpha males or females at HP who showed up with radical ideas or were willing to sign on to my crazy schemes. It was the quiet people, the ones who had sat and sometimes stewed over the way things were but who had never spoken up before. People who were good workers, but easy to ignore because the military model our companies follow (or used to follow . . .) expects that great ideas come only from our "leaders."

That's why I called an early version of this book *Lead from Below.* Now I see that it should have been *Lead from the Left, Lead from the Right, Lead from Wherever You Are, But Do It!*

If we don't do it, who will? If not now, then when?

ONE FOOT IN THE DOOR

My first year at HP, I hide out a lot. Radical, feminist, non-technical, female: how is this ever going to work? I read three or four spy novels a week, unconsciously trying to learn how to "pass" in a foreign country without discovery.

I am Hewlett Packard employee # 210834. I can't believe it. I'm inside! It's my first day of work, January 11, 1984. After years in the nonprofit sector, this is a miracle. With a doctorate in psychology, a master's in theology and comparative literature, and work experience as an actress, car mechanic, machinist, newspaper columnist, teacher, and college administrator, I have made it in the door. (I guess it helped to leave some of this off the resume, including the doctorate, as the manager who wanted to hire me suggested.)

I am the staffing manager at Santa Clara Division in Santa Clara, California, which makes measurement instruments, strange things like counters, analyzers, test equipment, and the atomic clock. They asked me why I wanted to work here. Each of them, in all ten interviews, over three days. Why do they ask such a thing? What do they really think a job candidate will say? I blah-blah-blahed about my love of recruiting, my fascination with engineering, etc., hoping my acting skills were kicking in.

Because the real reason I want to work here, the thing that really, really grabbed me, is that the toilets are so clean—

and I didn't have to clean them. The cool green sparkling enamel, the faint scent of pine, the lights that work, the toilet paper on the roll, with a backup roll on top. This luxury, I want it. This is the real reason I wanted to get a job here—any job.

I was thrilled that they couldn't tell at my first interview that I'd been cleaning toilets an hour before. As the director of the remote campus of a two-year electronics college that wasn't doing too well, my job involved doing whatever it took to keep the place running. The ex-cons who attended a rehab program on the site found it amusing to stick hoses under the door of my office and turn them on, and jam the toilets with whatever they could find, causing them to overflow. I spent a good deal of time in fear, and in water; and finally, when they shot all my windows out, I began looking for another job.

The morning of my first interview at HP there was another flooded toilet at the college. After filing a police report and chatting with the cops (again), I raced to the bathroom outside the local McDonald's and changed into a beautiful new suit—something that I imagined people wore in corporations. The suit worked, my answers worked, magic happened, and I'm here!

The suit, which I'm wearing again, feels very uncomfortable. The panty hose itch and so do all the additional waistbands: hose, slip, and skirt. Arrgghhh. I hate this drag! But it comes with the clean toilets and it's worth it, for now.

I'm thinking about my dissertation advisor, Peter Newton, and his brilliant article on the failure of the radical psychology movement in the '60s. One of the things he pointed out was that the Left was so invested in *looking* radical—with beads and beards or braless—that we completely alienated the very people we could have worked with to radically reorient psychology from focusing on "sick and crazy" people to focusing on the institutions that make people sick and crazy. Then we could have worked on the transformation of those institutions.

Now *that* would have been radical psychology, changing the institutions of social service, education, government, and commerce. But to do that, we would have had to wear suits, panty hose and bras, shave our legs and faces, and look like "respectable" citizens—and this we would not do.

I can remember the Junior League asking our radical women's group to come and talk because they didn't understand feminism. What we should have done was gone down to the thrift store and bought some Nordstrom secondhand clothes. But instead we went in combat boots and shaved heads, and the Junior League became very clear: Feminism was not for them!

All of which reminds me of the deeper reason I want this job, why I want into high tech. Why I have become a spy in the house of profit. While it seems like HP is the belly of the beast—from the perspective of my radical values—it also feels to me like the place to be to make the biggest difference

Radical Stand

PUT A STAKE IN
THE GROUND

for the planet. So this is where I'm taking my stand. This is where I'm putting my stake in the ground and saying, "I am going to make a difference *here*. I will not be swayed from my purpose. I will not be deflected. I will give it all I've got."

The old paradigm of the good, morally superior Church, and the evil, immoral, and rapacious Corporation has begun to break down for me anyway. This process began years ago as I and other women in divinity schools all over the country marched on behalf of superior women faculty members who had been refused tenure; filed lawsuits against sex and race discrimination in admissions; worked for the retention and promotion of women students and students of color; and began identifying the white and patriarchal dimensions of our religious traditions.

As the staff of women's centers linked to theological education, we share our experiences with each other and come to see that, like the churches at large, we depend on money from the very "evil" we deplore: big business. While I've been uneasy about this contradiction, based on what I've seen during my own fundraising, I'm horrified to learn that there are church fundraisers who keep demographic profiles on wealthy soon-to-be-widowed parishioners so as to be the first to comfort them. I also find that some funding sources for religious projects are the very same organizations that are deplored from the pulpit as exploitation. We learn from an experienced fundraising director that there is no money he would regard as too tainted to take—he believes that we transform money through the uses to which we put it. We ask, but what about our implicit sanction—a sanction the donor is certainly seeking—of how the money was made? We lose him at this point.

I continue to see ways in which the supposed do-good

sector isn't walking its talk. For example, one of the Protestant denominations wins a suit at the Supreme Court level affirming its right to discriminate based on gender. A woman had filed an Equal Employment Opportunity Commission (EEOC) complaint against the church for barring her from a job for which she was more qualified than the man to whom it was given. The catch was, the job had been advertised for men. The church—using money raised mostly from its female parishioners, as most of church money is—defends its right to discriminate, based on the constitutional separation of church and state. The church wins. Women lose.

As I personally march, protest, sit in, and file suit, I often fear what might happen to me as a result. But I also have the feeling that whatever does happen, I am doing what I am meant to do. I am trusting the spirit that moves me to speak the truth and take action on behalf of myself and of other women. I am "remembering Who I work for," taking courage from the fact that I have committed

Radical Stand

REMEMBER WHO
YOU WORK FOR

my life to the greater good. When I take this kind of radical stand, I know I am not working for my own small benefit, nor just for the benefit of this university—or this company or this nation. I am acting on behalf of something that transcends this time and place, something to which we have given many names but not enough attention.

In the end, no one shoots me and our work results in widespread changes in theological and higher education.

So, after working with the churches for more than a decade as a divinity student and as a director of the women's center for the nine theological schools of the Graduate Theological Union, I no longer see the religious sector as the conscience of the planet, nor the guardian of its future. There are too few checks and balances, both internally and externally, and consequently, there's too much unchecked corruption throughout the sector. Many wonderful friends continue to work for change within and through the religious sector. I applaud their vision and persistence. It is no longer my path.

The HP Way?

They talk a lot here about the HP Way, Bill Hewlett and Dave Packard's belief that people fundamentally want to do the right thing, and if you give them a supportive environment and the right tools, they will. But it seems to me that— much like the "way" of most of the religious institutions I've dealt with—the HP Way really means "married, two kids, churchgoing." As personified by Carol Love, one of the people on my interview team. The picture on her desk of her and her blond husband and two blond kids is in a heart-shaped frame, if you can believe it. During the interviews, I was sure she would be the one to keep me from getting the job. Somehow this didn't happen.

Luckily, I seem to be able to do the job. I supervise all aspects of recruiting the 110 engineers we've got to get in the door: selecting candidates, searching through the huge HP database, phone screening, on-site interviewing, handling travel logistics, making offers, getting new hires in place. The work is intense and we have barely the people we need to get it all done. Even so, it's easier than trying to end sexism in theological education with a budget of forty thousand dollars and fourteen volunteers, which was my job at the Graduate Theological Union in Berkeley.

I'm about four months into the job when Carol tells me she told the hiring manager after my interview, "If you don't hire her I'm going to quit. She's just what we need." At morning break, we walk outside and begin talking about our lives. She's dying inside that heart-shaped frame. Hasn't had an evening out on her own in years. Wants to join a group of women exploring their lives through their dreams.

Radical Move

RECRUIT CO-
CONSPIRATORS

Can't imagine how. It would be once a month. We talk about what it could mean in her life. She makes it happen.

She wants to know about my time as the first feminist news columnist in the country (at the *Capitol Times* in Madison, Wisconsin); my years as a socialist feminist hippie; the years in the peace, civil rights, and women's movements. She soaks up my story and begins to write completely new chapters in her own. In a few years I will have to call her to find out where I can do a sweat lodge and she will give me several alternatives, all with her personal assessment, along with a travel brochure of mystical journeys—personally, she's off to Machu Picchu.

So if Carol isn't the HP Way after all, perhaps it's a guy I'll call Bob. A total nerd—thin, pale, complete with plastic pocket protector, thick glasses, and an engineering project I can't understand. The quintessential HP employee, a man with no need to hide out. We talk now and then about nothing.

I'm just back from lunch one hot day and Bob's sitting at

the side of my desk. Can he talk to me? Of course, I say. He has something he wants to tell me that he's never told anyone else. He looks very uncomfortable, and I ask him if we should get a meeting room where we will have some privacy. With some relief, he agrees.

Bob and I walk over to the room. And then, with great hesitation, he shares with me his great secret. He feels he doesn't fit in at all and if HP really knew who he was, they wouldn't want him. I ask him why, imagining all kinds of things, but I'm completely unprepared for Bob's secret: he's Canadian, not American. He asks me what I think. I say I can really understand his feeling of not belonging, and tell him he's the personification of HP to me. I can't imagine anyone belonging if he doesn't. He's astonished. I go on to say I don't think being Canadian should be a reason for feeling like he doesn't belong. There are other Canadians. I name a few. And then I tell him a story that I also need to hear.

When I was directing the Center for Women and Religion, we had a retreat for the board, directors, work-study student staff, and the students we served. At some point, the question came up, Who is at the center of the Center? Oddly, the board thought the directors were; the directors thought the students were; the student staff thought the students were; the students thought the board of directors was. *No one experienced herself at the center.*

Bob and I muse on the question, What is this in us that has us always putting ourselves outside the circle of the select few that run things? Maybe the benefit of feeling "outside" is that we don't have to be responsible for what goes on. But I think a lot of us would be willing to be responsible, except at a deeper level we feel completely incapable and unable—for whatever reason. We have no sense of agency in our own lives. And this leads us to collude in our own powerlessness in ways that we never examine, beginning with never sharing our fears and our dreams with the people around us.

Standing outside the circle that decides things, we become spectators to our own lives. We're watching TV, have lost the remote, and can't change the channel. At best we're bored; at worst, depressed, suicidal, or homicidal. With no sense of agency in our own lives, we can never put down a stake, take a stand, act on what we care passionately about. With no stake, it becomes very difficult to feel anything at all, let alone feel something passionately.

I share with Bob some of my radical past, including the fact that my partner is a woman. He sees with great relief that there are things more strange than being Canadian. He wonders why I came to HP since I'm interested in changing the world. I tell him I think this is the place to do it, but I'm not sure how. This, he says, he can really understand. He leaves and I'm astonished: I have a new friend, Bob. Who looks like a real person to me now, not a nerd anymore.

Radical Move

RECRUIT CO-CONSPIRATORS

Amazing.

Coming Out of Hiding

Having managed to stay in the political closet for almost a year now, I'm beginning to relax a little, believing I'm not going to be suddenly fired. I no longer wear the suit, but comfortable slacks and blouses. One of the managers for whom I do employee relations assures me, "You look like one of us now. Like you work in a manufacturing division. Not like a corporate type."

One sunny Friday afternoon, I'm sitting at my desk staring at all the paperwork ahead of me when a guy I'll call Al, an alpha male R&D manager, comes into the office, throws his draft of an offer letter at my secretary, and barks, "Get this out by three o'clock or you're going to hear from me!" then stalks out. My secretary bursts into tears and runs to the ladies' room.

Without thinking, adrenaline pumping, I stalk Al to his office, corner him, and say low and firm, "Don't you ever treat one of my people like that again or we'll never help you with another hire. Do you understand me?" Astonished, Al replies, "What do you mean? What did I do?" He really has no idea.

Radical Stand

PUT A STAKE IN
THE GROUND

Radical Tool

TURN "ENEMIES"
INTO ALLIES

Unbeknownst to me, this is his style with everyone. Unbeknownst to him, not for much longer. I lay out for him what's happened, how it looks, how it feels, and the fact that my secretary is probably still in the ladies' room, sobbing. He feels awful, and later that afternoon comes in and apologizes to her.

A friendship with Al begins that day and grows with each confrontation.

Out on a Limb and Scaling Down

The next confrontation with Al occurs over recruiting

students for summer 1985. "So," I ask him, "how many summer students do you want? We're targeting minorities and this is a great opportunity for the division to balance our workforce." His face falls and he says, "Well, I'll take two minorities and then get me two smart ones." I reply, "How about four smart minorities?" He frowns. "C'mon, Barb, you know what I'm saying." "C'mon," I say back, "just give me a chance!" "Oh, go ahead," he sighs, "see what you can do. But if you can't get me at least two smart ones, the deal is off."

I want us not just to reach, but to far exceed the diversity hiring goals for our division's student program: one-third minority, one-third women, and one-third "other." Although we've never met the one-third-minority or one-third-women goal, I see no reason why we can't. A company this good ought to get more than its "fair share." Pestering the minority professional groups for candidates, my staff and I develop a candidate pool that is all minorities except for two Caucasians, both sons of HP employees. (We haven't actively recruited HP employees' kids—as is usually the case in the summer hire program—but we haven't turned them away either.) The pool's combined GPA is 3.8—the highest we've ever had—brought down from 3.9 by the two Caucasians.

I proudly show the candidate pool to my manager, Patricia Lingen, before I open it up to the hiring managers the next day. To my astonishment, Patricia is very worried. "This could cause a backlash—what's going to happen when our HP employees realize there are no slots left for their sons and daughters because you've filled them with minority kids?" She asks me to check with corporate headquarters about what to do. To my amazement, the word from Corporate is that the one-third minority is not only a goal but a ceiling in place to prevent employee backlash over their own kids not being hired! They have no advice on how to get out of the dilemma I've created and wish me luck.

I am freaking out. I go back to Patricia. She does not care about the issue in the way I do, but she doesn't want a backlash on her hands, and she cares about me. She asks me point-blank, "You really, really want us to exceed these goals, don't you?" I confirm that I do—I really, really do. She looks at me, puzzled. I space out, flash back . . .

I am seven years old. I have a terrible skin disease that lasts for two years. Covered with scabs and smeared with medicines that are purple, tar black, or pasty white, I am the "stinky girl" at school. The one never picked in Red Rover, Red Rover. I learn young about the cruelty we humans are capable of, and the loneliness and pain of being an outsider. I have only one friend I can count on to touch and play with me: the ocean.

Growing up a fundamentalist Protestant in Miami, Florida in the '50s, the only diversity I see are Catholics, who we somehow learn smell different from us and are going to take over the country with all their kids, and Jews, who are smarter but can be our friends because maybe some of it will rub off on us. Since I have given up on people and switched to books, none of this affects my relationships: I have none.

Besides the ocean, the only friend I ever make is a girl I meet during high school. We cross paths at church camp in the kitchen, where we are both working off our camp scholarships. Peeling and quartering green grapes for the salads of visiting dignitaries, we find we have a lot in common, both being outsiders and living mostly in our dreams of how to save the world from the cruelty we see around us.

We discover we've both picked the same small women's college as our first choice. Being bookworms, we have good grades and know we'll both get in. We decide to become room-mates and continue our plans for changing the world. When my father hears of this plan, he says, "No way. I'm not using my hard-earned money to send you up there to room with a Negro girl and get both of you killed." Then, as now, he's more tuned in to the news than I am. These are the years of Little Rock and the Birmingham bombing, and this parental stricture may well have saved my life. So I go to Florida State University instead, where I have a scholarship.

Through my church group at FSU, I get involved in an exchange program with Florida A.&M., the all-black college across town. Boys and girls pair up and go to the movies. I have several painfully awkward evenings with my date, as we go around town and campus, the objects of curious—and more often hostile—stares and remarks. Another activity I get involved in is teaching in the "freedom schools," which, I learn years later, are a key strategy in the early Civil Rights movement. Black children boycott their public schools, forc-ing the school district to lose its matching revenues from the federal government, and come to our freedom school, where we teach them what we are also learning about Harriet Tubman, Sojourner Truth, and each other's hair.

One bright and early morning, our youth minister, a frail old woman named Mrs. Wilson, calmly tells us that we have received bomb threats and should keep our eyes open for white men in cars cruising too close to the school. For the first time in my life, I feel that I am in a moment in history that matters, one of those moments when life invites you to decide who you're going to be. And while I am very scared, I decide that whatever happens, I am doing what I was meant to do. I don't discover till several years later that I am part of a much larger Civil Rights movement . . .

Radical Stand

REMEMBER WHO
YOU WORK FOR

Patricia is talking. I snap back to the mess I seem to have created here, much as I hate to focus on it. It's late evening and I ask her to say again what she's been suggesting. In a masterful move that I will later turn into a tool called "scaling down," Patricia points out that our problem, violating Corporate's ceiling on proportion of minority to white candidates, is showing up at the *division* level of the candidate pool: only two white kids among dozens of minorities and women.

Like Einstein, who pointed out that you can't solve a problem on the level at which it is created, Patricia asks, "What if we scale down to the *hiring-manager* level? We don't need to advertise the ethnicity, gender, or GPA of the entire division candidate pool. We never have before. Why don't we just present each hiring manager with three or four matches for their summer job requisition: one or two of the minorities, and one or both of the Caucasians. That way, we get below the 'ceiling' and the managers feel they have some choice."

Radical Tool

SCALE DOWN

Thus, "scaling down" is born. Scaling down is about

changing perspective so the problem becomes either soluble or invisible. It's like flying so low, you're not on anyone's radar screen—and your radical acts aren't in anyone's face.

I look at Patricia, amazed at this brilliant strategy. And at the fact that she's still sitting with me this late at night in my sinking ship. This isn't an issue she is passionate about. But she *cares* about me. This is an important lesson. Through friendship, I am adding skills to my base capability. These skills may even come from people who don't share my values, but they are willing to share their skills because they care about me. I don't think Patricia would have gone to the mat for minority hiring, but she

Radical Move

TAP THE
STRENGTH OF
YOUR
RELATIONSHIPS

has gone to the mat for me. So she racked her brains and came up with this scaling-down solution. Brilliant.

With no backlash at all, our managers hire twenty-eight minorities, and two nonminorities. At the end of the summer, our managers vote this summer-hire program the best we've ever had: the kids are brighter and more innovative. One of the innovations is the kids' refusal to have the traditional picnic where the managers prepare lunch for them. They insist on preparing a thank-you lunch for the managers instead. The food comes from eleven cultures and could have fed the entire division.

After the summer, Al is so thrilled with the work and the teamwork of his four smart minority students, he becomes the HP campus manager at a minority college we target as a source of minority hires. He does this in addition to his Ivy League recruiting responsibilities.

He comes back from his first interviewing trip to the minority college. Our meeting is at 10:00 A.M., but he's at my desk two hours early, quite agitated. "I can't fill out these interview reports," he says. "These kids are carrying two, sometimes three jobs, supporting parents, kids—you name it. On top of a full-time course load. They are incredible managers, able to prioritize quickly, think on their feet. They're ten times more mature than my Ivy League students. And they're just as smart. They could answer all my questions. But their grades don't tell the story of how smart they are.

Radical Move

**BUILD YOUR
CADRE**

"Look at Jose, here," he says. "He's got C's his first two years of math. Then his junior year he gets a scholarship and can quit his jobs and suddenly it's A's. Even though his third-year math class builds on the foundation of two years of C classes. See! It proves it, these C's are really A's. So I'm just going to fill in this report with A averages on all of them. They are all capable, they just don't have the financial support the rich kids are getting. If I put down the C's, they'll never even get the first interview. If I put A's, they will. "So this is to let you know I'm going to put A averages on the interview reports."

Radical Tool

**TURN "ENEMIES"
INTO ALLIES**

I know exactly what Al is pointing at and I am almost in tears to feel the movement this guy has made from number-one bigot to number-one advocate in a matter of months. I tell him so. I tell him I love him. And then, even though I am upset myself at the situation he's painted so poignantly, I let him know my misgivings about his solution. If it's ever discovered that the grades he's entered are false, the kids will be considered the liars, not him. I tell him I'm going to call a friend I trust at Corporate, to see what he thinks.

When I get off the phone, Al and I arrive at a compromise. Al will put no grades at all down on the interview reports. Instead, he writes, "Call recruiter for more details on this outstanding student." He gets calls, and because he's also an Ivy League recruiter, and known not to be a "bleeding heart" like myself and others in the affirmative action circles, he's got more credibility. His students are hired.

I spend almost three years at Santa Clara Division and far exceed the affirmative action goals. As a result, I am promoted to the corporate headquarters to run recruiting HP-wide. But before I can wrap my head around the new job, another new job enters my life.

Chapter 2

IN THE BELLY OF THE BEAST

I have lost many of the radical friends of my pre-HP days, who think anyone working for a corporation has sold out. So why am I here? Why do I stay?

i am in the new Corporate job a few weeks when I receive the call I have been dreaming of for years: I am going to be a mother. An adoption lawyer has a hard-to-place baby coming and no parents lined up. Are we interested?

A baby is considered hard to place when s/he's born with a disability, is racially mixed, or is African American. That children of color are "hard to place" makes us crazy. We have specified that we want a child of color, with or without so-called "disabilities." Our thinking is this: Why should we conceive children when there are so many without parents? And why should we get a white and/or healthy child for whom it is much more likely parents can be found, when our goal is to parent kids who won't otherwise have any?

Our child is coming in a week and is African American. Her mother has had no prenatal care, so it is unknown whether there are disabilities.

I am nervous about the reactions of my own family of origin, and have not told them. My late grandfather once bragged to me of his Ku Klux Klan affiliation, and although my folks and most of my extended family—who live three thousand miles away—are very liberal for the South, still, we are all from the South!

Our newborn daughter arrives in the arms of her birth mother and her aunt. We talk about our lives together. They are thrilled that I was once—though just for a night—Angela Davis's bodyguard.

Our daughter is beautiful. We've never been happier! Crazy as it sounds even to me, I'm also thrilled with the medical plan that covers her care through my company, so far superior to any coverage she would have received through the welfare system or the pathetic health plans I was on before joining HP. And let's face it: this is another reason I'm at HP. My previous six-thousand-dollars-a-year salary with no benefits was a shaky foundation on which to start a family.

I call my middle sister, Betsy, to get her thoughts on what to do about the folks. She advises a letter so they can have their shock in private and say their first thoughts without witnesses. I write the letter and send off a picture of the three of us.

My parents call, thrilled for us. Two days later, a huge box of baby clothes arrives, along with a bouquet toasting the newest member of the family.

How have my parents come to embrace this unlikely grandchild? How did Al become my best minority recruiter? Is it possible we humans can change so profoundly? Is there something in us that knows the species is doomed unless we do? I'm beginning to wonder if there's a bigger movement, a species-level movement, transpiring through us all.

Finding the "Deviants"

When my new manager recruited me, he said, "You've got so many ideas of how to change things—do it!"

So here I am and I'm panicked. What if I can't? This is Corporate! In just three years I'm managing recruiting for a company I believe I barely got into. What if they find out how much I don't know what I'm doing? Or what if I just screw up royally? It's all so visible up here!

Luckily for me, Emily Duncan has just joined HP. Emily, a new diversity manager, is stunningly gorgeous, six feet tall, dark chocolate, with a shaved head molded like Cleopatra's. I know she will be an ally in figuring out what to do, but I'm paralyzed about how to approach her with my ideas. I've got the high school uglies in a big way. My mind is saying, "Emily's one of the beautiful, popular girls and she'll never be my friend."

The situation is too important, I can't stay stuck in this place, so I tell her I'm stuck in the uglies, we laugh, and I get over myself.

Together, we look at our affirmative action hiring. In every category, we are hiring fewer people than the U.S. Department of Labor statistics suggest could be HP's share, given the demographics on people graduating with various scientific degrees. For ex-

Radical Move

RECRUIT CO-CONSPIRATORS

ample, if the bureau's data show that 3 percent of recent electrical engineering grads are black, we should be hiring 3 percent of blacks for our electrical engineering openings.

Worse yet, our statistics are based on the availability of electrical engineers. That may have been the old HP, but today more than half our hiring is computer scientists, a field with far more women and minority graduates than electrical engineering. When we recompute availability based on the numbers of computer-science graduates, we discover we are even further from our affirmative action goals.

What can we do? We set ourselves the preposterous task of exceeding our goals in three years. Emily's genius is to start with what we have and move on from there. I often overlook what we have in my enthusiasm to get us where I think we should be.

So what do we actually *have*? If we stop looking at the big picture—which is discouraging because we're so far from where we want to be—and scale down from the aggregate, we can see that there are small clusters of HP hiring managers, staffing folks, and affirmative action representatives all over the country who "get it." Without scaling down, everybody looks alike and everybody is failing. But when we look case by case, we see some startling successes.

Radical Tool

SCALE DOWN

These successes are people whom we will later recognize as "positive deviants," people with the same resources as their neighbors but who deviate from them in some positive way. In this case, the norm is managers who don't hire a fair percentage of women and minorities. Managers who deviate from that norm and do have a balanced staff are showing a positive trait. And the way to spread the practices of these positive deviants is to amplify them.

Finding and then amplifying people inside the organization who already embody and are living out the "desired future state"—or want to—is counterintuitive. Why? Because most change efforts are conceived at the organizational level of scale. At this level, you see the organization as a whole, and in need of change. Intuitively, it feels like if the organization were "already doing it," then there wouldn't be a problem. And at this level, you can't see those who don't embody the problem.

It's only as you scale down, using the filter of "desired future state," that you begin to find those who embody it already, or who want to. And as we've seen elsewhere, these are often not the "leaders" or "alpha employees" in the current organization (who are being rewarded for making things the way they are)—an additional reason they're overlooked.

No, somehow we seem to much more comfortably default to a mechanical model, one based on the Prussian military: The lines of command are very tight, closely coupled, and the way you get from A to B is that the person at the top of the pyramid says, "March!" and everybody marches from A to B. Supposedly.

The mechanistic military model works best when, as in the Prussian army, the top brass are better educated, have privileged critical information, and are highly respected by the uneducated peasant classes who work for them. It doesn't work so well with knowledge workers who are often better educated than "the top" and may be tactically better informed about decisions that need to be made.

Another reason the military model breaks down in our new economy is that, increasingly, we who work in corporations aren't a neat hierarchy of tightly stacked layers. We're more like a seething mass, and the corporations we work in have become a complex, teeming living system, full of vectors of energy (whether they be people or projects or priorities). Everything is going in every direction.

How then do you get from A to B? You find the vectors of energy that are *already* pointing toward B and amplify them.

They are your positive deviants. By finding your models for change *inside* your organization, you are accomplishing two crucial things. First, you are dumping the traditional organization-development model where you (or, more often, outside consultants) go in and focus on a community's *deficits*. In this traditional model, kin to the military model, you are the expert and the people involved in the actual work don't know anything.

Radical Tool

AMPLIFY POSITIVE
DEVIANCE

The new model says, "We're not the expert, we don't know anything. Within your community you have the answers, so let's understand together what they are." The idea is that in any community, there's someone who has already moved from A to B, who's already embodying the desired future state.

The second thing you accomplish when you find your "experts" within your own company is that you don't get the antibody effect that comes with bringing in outsiders—consultants or their latest and greatest models for success. Because the corporation is a living system—it's made up of human beings, after all—when a foreign agent invades, it reacts. That's what got our radical feminist group in trouble with the Junior League. We looked, sounded and probably smelled like invaders.

But when you come in looking like the system, something compatible, you won't get attacked.

This is related to a principle I will learn later and put to use at HP: "Tweak, don't toss." It means make small changes, do what's doable, and do what wants to be done. Get under the antibody threshold.

So Emily and I, ignoring those managers who aren't committed to diversity hiring, scale down and focus on those who are. We find our positive deviants and amplify them. How?

Radical Tool

TWEAK,
DON'T TOSS

First, we bring them together into a cross-business, personnel-related grassroots community; they name themselves the "Affirmative Action Network." Working with them, Emily and I identify what they are doing that's different from the norm. Among other things, they are networking with each other by phone, e-mail and occasional visits, and passing on the names of good minority and women job candidates. They are even providing jobs to each other's minority employees who want to transfer.

Then we amplify these positive deviants. We feature their "best practices" month after month in the recruiting newsletter. When necessary, we talk with their managers to make sure these folks are given time and travel expenses to attend important minority-recruiting conferences. Out of our own

Radical Tool

AMPLIFY
POSITIVE DEVIANCE

budgets we sponsor the ones who are interested to attend additional minority-recruitment training. Together we identify the behaviors, processes, and infrastructure that have made them successful, then we pass on these keys to success through newsletter articles and by giving regional workshops.

Finally, Emily and I approach their managers and lobby for our wonderful deviants to be rewarded for their best practices and their participation in the group by being granted stock options. Their managers agree, and—for the first time ever—a cross-business grassroots group gets stock options in recognition of the importance of their contribution.

We exceed our goals in two years.

Positive vs. Negative

Although Emily and I are identifying and amplifying our positive deviants, that isn't the term used for what we are doing. The practice won't be popularized until the mid-1990s, when Jerry Sternin of Save the Children begins writing about his experience fighting childhood malnutrition in rural Vietnam.

The story starts with a string of frustrated attempts to end hunger, attempts that for one reason or another don't work. Then one of the relief workers remarks that not *all* the children in these villages are malnourished. In fact, there are some children of very poor families who are actually flourishing. So the community decides to study what is going on for these children that is different from what's happening for the malnourished children.

And they find that when the parents of the flourishing children go down to the rice paddies to pick rice, they also collect tiny shrimp and crabs the size of one joint of one finger and add these to the rice. They also throw in the greens from sweet potato tops. Because of these casual additions to the pot, the children of these parents are getting more vitamins, minerals, protein, and roughage.

So Save the Children helps these parents teach the others how to add nutrition to their kids' diets. And they prove that the conventional wisdom—which holds that these foods are not appropriate for children and may even be harmful to them—is false. The "positive deviant" parents become the trainers for transforming the system. So you have neighbors training neighbors. And within two years, 80 percent of the children in the project are no longer malnourished. Four years later, an outside auditor verifies that the number has grown to 90 percent. The community sustains the best practices that support its life.

This approach gets expanded to other villages in Vietnam—more than 250 in all—and to poor villages in Bangladesh, Bhutan, Mali, Egypt, Mozambique, and Nepal. The answer isn't always the same—sometimes the extra ingredients are peanuts or seeds or dried fish. Sometimes the children are being fed several meals a day instead of just two. But the process is the same. And the solution is sustainable because it comes from the people themselves. It is not necessary to provide the villages with money or jobs or sacks of grain in order to help these children. In fact, nothing from the "outside" is needed at all, except a little coaching.

My own experience with "amplifying positive deviance" is an eye-opener.

During my years as an activist in the '60s and '70s, the primary strategy I was engaged in I would now dub "amplifying *negative* deviance," though we didn't think of it that way at the time. We went out and found the worst offenders—the biggest racists, the biggest sexists—identified them, and held press conferences to embarrass them. We did whatever we could to make a bad example of them. But all that really did was amplify them. Which made them stronger. And mad. They fought back. And if they had the money for guns, they'd shoot you down.

At the Center for Women and Religion in Berkeley, in the mid-'70s, we looked at the presidents of the nine schools that made up the Graduate Theological Union and singled out the ones we believed to be doing the least for women. We embarrassed them, pointed out the flaws in their thinking from our own theological perspectives, accused their denominations of oppression of women, and on and on. But these were the guys who were funding our center. And they didn't like what we were doing. Our funding from them got smaller each year, and from some, threatened to dry up completely.

That's when I had this great awakening: We were going to get wiped out if we kept this up. So we changed our tack. We began looking for the presidents who were acting bravely, out of the box, to empower women and minorities. We celebrated them, invited them to speak to the others about their strategies and tactics, visions and values. We even focused in on the "worst" of our earlier detractors, found one thing he did right, in our opinion, and amplified this one positive behavior. He eventually became a big fan, commending us publicly for our years of work on behalf of women.

Radical Tool

AMPLIFY
POSITIVE DEVIANCE

I am not saying there's no role for amplifying the negative. There is—and it's a crucial one—but I've found it's less frequently useful than my Leftist training would have had me believe.

For one thing, I've watched myself get so excited about amplifying the negative that I not only get righteous (and therefore blind) about my own position, I overlook progress, signs of change, and the positive in the opposition. So for me, amplifying the negative is now a strategy of last resort (unless I slip, which I do a lot).

Looked at theoretically, amplifying the negative is crucial for identifying a problem at the front end. For example, it was very important at the beginning of the Civil Rights movement to identify and distinguish what was racist from what was okay. And this had to be done with a great deal of passion or it wouldn't have gotten noticed.

There will always be a need for making distinctions (via amplifying the negative) because once the culture—whether it be a family, a small town, a nation, or the world—understands one level of the problem, it will need to understand the next deeper level. For example, right now, the things I am realizing about racism by raising two African American children are at a much more subtle level than the segregation and open hatred I saw when I was younger. If I don't shout about what I am seeing now, no one who's not a victim of it can hear or see that it exists.

At the front end of making these new distinctions about subtle racism and the hurtful and diminishing behaviors of others, I do sometimes amplify the negative. But I try to do it as a last resort. First, I try to remember to ask myself, How do

I want to spend my time? Do I want to put my precious, finite energy into trying to stamp out the negative? Or do I want to squeeze the negative out of existence by growing the positive? For me, the choice is definitely amplifying the positive. I don't fault anyone who finds the alternative a better match for their values and inclinations. Indeed, I find that at the level of strategy, amplifying the negative is a necessary and absolutely critical step in differentiating what we want to keep in the present as we head toward the future and what we want to jettison. It's just not the role in the revolution that I want to be my primary role right now.

Temptation

I am invited to interview several times for promotion from my recruiting job to a personnel manager job. I turn down these invitations, because I don't like the work of a personnel manager: solving all the people problems that no one else can.

One day, though, a friend I'll call Helen, the personnel manager at one of our largest sites, picks me up for lunch. She has three small children and I'm amazed at how clean her car is. Ours is a mess with just one. "Oh," she says breezily, "they vacuum the company cars every morning. It's the best thing about being a personnel manager!"

"You mean if I take one of these jobs, and get one of these cars, they'll clean it every morning?" "Sure, you bet!" she says with a grin. I begin to rethink the personnel manager job.

I say yes to the next invitation to interview. And not a minute too soon. The car is about to get a lot messier.

Black and White, Again

Two years after we adopt our daughter, I am holed up in a motel in a small town in the Louisiana bayou with our baby boy, who's been with me since he was two hours old. He's now three days old. I have to live here for a week to prove to the state of Louisiana that this isn't a kidnapping. I'm nervous because he's African American and I'm Caucasian. The nurses from the hospital are great. They give me lots of free supplies and call me daily to check on us. The motel staff are wonderful, too, and help in every way they can. But having grown up around here, I know about the bodies that have disappeared into the bayou and I am unable to shake my fear.

One afternoon I'm holding the baby while I listen to my voice mail. It's the director of HP Labs, offering me a job. As I listen, a helicopter lands outside the motel room and armed men hop out. I am sure we are going to be killed. I hang up on voice mail, take the baby to the bathroom, lock the door, and get ready to dial 911, thinking it will probably be too late. An hour passes. Nothing happens. Then I hear the helicopter again. I leave the bathroom and look out the window. They're gone. I call the front desk. No one knows who these people were, why they came, or why they left—probably a "training exercise" is all anyone says.

Could that be true? I sit with my new son, marveling that the world may have changed so much that my son and I are a nonevent. With that thought, I realize how much I have dreaded this trip, how afraid I've been, how completely I've surrendered to the possibility that we could be killed.

The whole time I've been here, I've been surrounded by

love and support, but I've felt like I'm being stalked by a great lumbering presence on my left side, just out of view. I know on some level it's related to the lynchings and rapes and murders that have been committed here, to the three hundred years of my people brutalizing my son's people.

So my fear—which is vivid and visceral and huge—*is* based on real experience, but that experience is in the past. There is nothing in the current situation to support it. My commitment to the bad old days of the South is preventing the real positive in the current moment from defeating the real negative in the past. And if I don't allow the present to defeat the past, how will a future different from the past ever emerge?

I resolve to commit myself to the present. The fear continues to stalk me, but it's old stuff and doesn't have to get me now.

I anchor myself with voice mail. I call Patricia, my manager in my first HP job. I ask her, "What if I can't do this personnel manager job? The woman who just left it was completely burned out, working eighty-hour weeks. Should I be taking this on with a two-year-old and a brand new baby?" I tell her that the main thing that got me interested was that the Cheerios on the car floor will be vacuumed up by someone else.

Patricia says, "Take it, Waugh. Look at it this way: Even if you bomb at the job completely, it will take them at least a year to figure it out, another year to do anything about it, and meantime, you can be riding around in that nice clean car."

With this counsel, I call and accept the job.

Chapter 3

A JOB WITH A CAR

*I am constantly amazed at the powerlessness and dependency I/
we manifest in the face of authority. Is it wired into our DNA?
Or do years of childhood dependency socialize us into it, burn it
into the brain's circuits? I can't answer for humankind, but I do
know in my own case, I must take inventory daily to catch where
I've fallen yet again into resignation and powerlessness in the
face of someone or some event I reflexively assume can decide
how it's going to be for me and those I care about.*

I start the new job in January of 1990. It's tough. I am personnel manager for HP Labs, the central research lab that is
responsible for finding and inventing the technologies that
will keep HP competitive. The nine hundred engineers—over
half of whom have advanced degrees—work on coming up
with what the company will be selling three to five years
from now. These are major-league players. Counting the three
hundred support people, there are twelve hundred HP Labs
employees in all and we are spread around the world, from
Palo Alto and Boston to Japan, China, Israel, and England.

The work is standard personnel stuff, covering the spectrum from wages, salaries, leaves, and recruiting to crisis
management. But it's far from a standard job. As my prede-
cessor warned me, it is eighty hours a week. Thank god for
my babies—I *can't* give that much time to this job, so a kind
of balance is enforced.

Even so, one evening after work I am so tired from sleep-less nights and stressful days that I have to stop the car just ten minutes and one freeway exit from home and take a nap before I can keep going.

Tough. As I expected, I get all the people problems that no one else can solve. There are lots of guidelines to help, but often it's my call in the end. The hardest is to figure out how to let people go; the most frightening, the two stalkings; the most frustrating, the sexism that to me is obvious, to my managers, not.

One morning, I am in a meeting discussing a fairly important employee dispute and I notice—not for the first time—that I'm the only woman there, this time sitting with ten men: eight male managers and two male lawyers. We are reviewing a female engineer's complaint about a male colleague. The situation is a little unusual, but it's clear to me that we're looking at sexual discrimination. They don't see it. I ask them to consider reversing the gender in the room. What if there were eight women managers, two women lawyers, and a male personnel manager in this room? What would they see then? They don't really get it, but they are now profoundly uneasy—what am I really saying here?

I am driving home that afternoon, replaying the scene. Suddenly, I'm attacked by the Voice of Reason: "Are you crazy? Facing down the entire management team, everybody you work for? Do you understand that this was a career decision? How stupid can you get? This is your job on the line. At least the employee you were standing up for has a technical degree—she can get another job a lot easier than you can! What are you thinking? You have kids to support!"

I can feel the tears of exhaustion and despair welling up—and then I "hear" another voice, quieter, calm: "Who do you work for? Do you really think you work for all these boys? They are your brothers, your sons, your father. You do not work for them. You work for me! It is I who will give you your performance review. So, I have just two questions: Did you do what you thought was right? Did you do your best?"

I calm down, and respond aloud as the traffic seems to slow all around me. "Yes and yes." "Then," says the voice, "go home and rest. The rest of it is none of your business." "But what about my job?" I ask. "Have you ever been without enough to eat?" the voice asks. "Or even without a job?" "No and no."

To their enormous credit, my brothers/sons/father decide to boot the case up a level, given that we can't agree, even though it is their prerogative to override me. For reasons I am never privy to, the case is decided in favor of the woman.

That voice is my soul speaking; it is my anchor and my compass. It reminds me Who I really work for. If I had thought I really worked for any of those guys in that meeting—and as a matter of fact, I worked for most of them; every one of them had input into my performance evaluation, which is always a good measure of who you work for—I probably would have killed myself after that meeting. It was

Radical Stand

REMEMBER WHO
YOU WORK FOR

hopeless. But I don't work for them. I work for the greater good, for the promise of Hewlett-Packard, which demands that I do the right thing and make a contribution to the world. And every one of those guys at that meeting respects that.

The fact is, if you work for "them," it's much more difficult to be in loyal opposition. Because the whole idea of working for someone is that you support their intention and their goals, whatever they are. Whereas, if you work for spirit—the spirit of HP or the Great Spirit or God or however you think of it—you are at certain points going to have to say, "This is wrong" or "There is another way to look at this" or "This is not the only way to think about this." And the moment you say that, you are putting a stake in the ground and clearing the path for action.

Radical Stand

PUT A STAKE IN
THE GROUND

As the months go by and I am faced with more and more personnel problems, it's a revelation to me to see that HP has its own bell curve—we have all the problems that are happening outside our high-minded corporate walls. However, in my experience we handle them a lot better. Unlike the environment within the churches or academia where I've worked before, here there is a foundation of decency that you can rely on. You may have to risk your job to discover it, but when I have, it proves to be in place every time.

I don't know why this sense of decency prevails, but so far, in my experience, it has.

Is it because the civil rights laws *do* apply here, unlike the situation with the churches? Is it because there is enough to go around? (But even when there wasn't enough, Bill and

Dave didn't go to layoffs. They imposed 10 percent pay cuts for everyone and gave everybody but managers a day off every two weeks to make up for it.) Is it because this is a community? Not just a big machine, with each of us a lowly cog, but a community of people who care for each other in some fashion that doesn't obtain outside? Is this why I feel "family" when I see the HP badge on someone?

Strength in Numbers

The chair of the third HP Technical Women's Conference is Laurie Mittelstadt, an HP Labs engineer. She asks me to be on her advisory board and to help her put the conference together. I agree. This conference matters.

The first Technical Women's Conference (TWC), chaired by HP Labs engineer Darlene Solomon in 1988, brought together women whose voices were lost in the majority male culture at HP. In those days, women engineers in high tech represented a token presence, though their numbers were growing.

When women (or minorities) are distributed across a large population and isolated in departments that are otherwise all male (or any other majority), we have little influence and have a difficult time being heard or getting credit for our contributions. We are tokens. Rosabeth Moss Kanter discusses the phenomenon of tokenism in her landmark book *Men and Women of the Corporation.* Tokens burn out and do not change the system. The goal of tokens who want to make a difference, then, is to aggregate and become a group, a big enough group so as to become a minority because minority groups can and do change things.

With some instinctive knowledge of these truths, a steering committee of HP women organized the first TWC

Radical Move

BUILD
YOUR CADRE

Radical Tool

SCALE UP

and created the model that would last for over a decade: workshops and papers to showcase and develop women technically, in our careers, as stewards of the planet, and as a network, all the while demonstrating the value of women employees in general and the value of this gathering in particular to the bottom line of the company. That first year, four hundred women met— on a Saturday, since the company did not regard the meeting as work related. However, CEO John Young did show up and give the keynote.

That conference, like the one we are planning now in 1991, is crucial for the women at HP. It brings together isolated women engineers and other professionals so we can scale up and see our situation from a broader perspective, see our problems are not unique. It connects and empowers us.

The first big issue we face is that this year we want to hold the conference on company time. The TWC is clearly work-related, whether or not our management sponsors see it that way. To get management to see the light, we are going to have to speak their language. And to do that, I first have to change my own mind-set—an old left-wing legacy—that says, "Of course HP doesn't want to sponsor women meeting and comparing notes about what the company is doing to us." I have to assume instead that of course HP wants to do the right thing. We just have to show them why this *is* the right thing.

So we reframe the context of the conference. Instead of presenting it to management as an event that benefits women, we present it as an event that benefits HP, that is in the service of company values and goals. We focus on the benefits to HP of supporting its women employees in their professional development and in their community. We point out that the conference is not only an employee-development tool but an employee-retention tool. And an excellent one, too: it's pretty cheap, it's something the target audience wants, and it works!

Radical Tool

REFRAME THE CONTEXT

Luckily, we have incredibly wonderful women with a lot more credibility than I to explain this to management. There are really solid, outstanding women engineers, like Darlene Solomon—who, on any level you measure her, is your quintessential ideal employee—who really wants the conference and is willing to sit down and quite reasonably make our case. It's good for me to recognize when I'm *not* the one who should go in and tackle the "opposition."

Radical Move

BUILD YOUR CADRE

This is another aspect of building your cadre: sharing the opportunity to lead. When we do this, we discover that the extent to which people own a project is the extent to which they invest their time and energy to make it succeed.

Besides, I'm not real coolheaded on this particular subject. I mean, this whole notion that we shouldn't meet on company time just undoes me. Laurie and I go around ranting, "Are you kidding? Every single day here is a men's conference. We just want two days in the year for women!"

Eventually, we make enough noise and we win our point. We can have two workdays to hold the TWC.

(Reflecting on this TWC a few years later, Laurie appears on the front page of a section of the *Wall Street Journal* saying, "Every single day at HP is a men's conference...we just wanted two days for women!" Oh no, I think. "You've had it," the Voice of Reason thunders in my head. I am sure someone from somewhere is going to lower the boom. But in the article, HP comes across as a company that supports people speaking their truth, even if it isn't flattering. So even this works in the service of the company.)

Laurie and I decide to invite Anne Firth Murray, founder and director of the Global Fund for Women, to be a keynote speaker. We ask her to challenge us to think about our success: "Success for what?" I am a little afraid of doing this, as I am every time I bring my radical past (or present) into work. What if "Success for what?" ticks women off? What if Anne's outspoken beliefs about patriarchy and women's oppression offend someone? But I am even more afraid of living in a world where women can't speak up.

When I prepare my remarks to introduce Anne, I remind everyone that members of the Hewlett and Packard families were founding donors of the Global Fund for Women. Compelled by the prospect of the deep and expectant listening of eight hundred women, I decide I will say that I believe global companies should define corporate citizenship *not* as something we do in the mile-and-a-half radius around the factories where we operate, but as something we do on the entire planet—which, for a global company, *is* the neighborhood. My dream of HP raising the bar on what it means to be a corporate citizen begins to take shape with this talk.

With voice mail, working at all hours in all time zones, Laurie, a woman who is a senior engineering manager at HP Labs, and I network all over the company for the self-organizing subcommittees, who invite speakers and line up the conference site. In crisis after crisis, we discover support from unexpected places all over the company.

Next crisis? We need money. A lot of it, to pay advances for the hotel and speakers. And we need it long before we can possibly collect enough conference registration fees. Will Corporate front us the money, given that the TWC is a diversity retention tool?

No. No part of Corporate will fund us.

What to do? With a few days left before the hotel cancels our reservation, I pour out our woes to the HP Labs controller, Andrew Liu, already a good friend, and afterward one of my best friends in the whole company. Seeing the right thing to do, he signs for the large advances—and figures out how to do it above board—even though he is risking exposure if we have a shortfall.

Radical Move

TAP THE STRENGTH
OF YOUR
RELATIONSHIPS

And one cold, dark night, it looks like a shortfall is exactly what we're going to have. Laurie comes by my office on her way out the door, stricken. Our care-

fully planned conference has been cancelled due to companywide expense controls. We will lose all our deposits.
All our planning will be for nothing. Is there anything I
can do?

I can't think of anything, but I automatically reach for
the phone. I call a former boss at Corporate, now a good
friend. He says, "Better believe it. It's canceled. Don't fight it.
You'll just look like you're not a team player."

This isn't the answer I want, so I keep calling. I reach
my current boss, the director of HP Labs, on his car phone.
He's completely sympathetic. A street fighter, he kicks into
action. He has a meeting the next morning with Dean Morton,
the chief operating officer of the company. He'll ask Dean if
they can make a special case for this conference. Frank reports back that he didn't even have to argue the case: Dean
Morton declared this conference an exception. We are on!

Eight hundred people come to our two-day conference,
double the number who attended the first one. Afterward,
Laurie Mittelstadt leaves me a "picture" voice mail, as she
will do many more times over the next ten years. In these
she describes all facets of her own experience of our latest
kaleidoscopic event. Laurie's pictures:

- "Walking into the conference room, feeling awe in
  the company of almost a thousand women who were
  kind of like me—a conference that makes insiders
  of outsiders, a place to fit in for those of us living in
  a world where we don't fit in.
- "The farmer-engineer woman in overalls and boots,
  the techno-marketers in their red suits with bows

around their necks, the feminine marketers in their high-heels and plunging necklines, the engineers like me in brand-new suits.

- "Dean Morton coming to the podium, sweating with nervousness, opening with a great sigh and the words 'This must be how you feel'—and being unable to continue because of the roar of applause.

- "The latticework with flowers in front of the urinals in the men's rooms that we've converted to women's rooms for the day.

- "Knowing that I can walk up to anyone here, describe my work, hear that it is cool, and get help if I need it.

- "Finding an instant network of whom to call across the company [long before the Internet and posted org charts are available].

- "A woman who had decided not to be an R&D manager changes her mind after hearing one of the speakers. Other women also decide to take a chance, to go into management, to make that phone call.

- "Learning that the lessons learned are not unique to women but are human in scale."

After the conference we apply to Catalyst, a prestigious national advocacy organization for professional women, to be considered for their coveted annual award for positive change on behalf of women. We win it, making this the first time the Catalyst Award has been given to a grassroots group. Our CEO flies to New York to be filmed accepting the prize. We sit in the audience for the awards ceremony. When asked how he helped make this conference happen, John Young declares, "I did nothing but get out of the way!"

Over the next decade, thousands more HP women all over the world will join to produce these conferences. Soon, the TWC becomes an annual regional event that opens with meetings organized by different business sectors and attended by the sector vice president and his or her staff. At these meetings, the major business, technology, and marketing issues of the sector are presented, and the women present their ideas, questions, and proposals. They are challenged to take issues back to their divisions and come up with ideas and innovations to create breakthrough solutions to them.

Besides getting a chance to meet the vice president their division reports to, women network among themselves, often recruiting each other for business and technology teams and projects. This results in cross-functional experience, job transfers, and often promotions. Retention rates increase.

The core premise and benefit of the conference is women talking business. For example, at one of these gatherings, two women start a discussion that results in developing new technology for a chemical-analysis system that involves the materials and manufacturing know-how of thermal-ink-jet technology.

After a decade of Technical Women's Conferences, HP's company culture will be radically transformed into one where women can fully contribute. HP women become a voice, a presence, and equal partners with male colleagues for success and change.

At the same time, HP will become the first company on the Fortune 200 to be able to really "see" the best candidate for CEO—and not see just gender. Carly Fiorina will take over as HP's CEO on July 19, 1999. Coincidence that this happens in the only Fortune 200 with a Technical Women's Conference? I don't think so.

The Listening of the Deaf

Out of the TWC experience, I am invited to help with the Deaf and Hard of Hearing Forum, a network of about 125 HP employees, and in 1993 I am asked to keynote their conference.

Here's a situation where I am truly a minority, awkward, painfully aware of my differentness, my inadequacy. I plead with the organizers to find someone else in HP who is better qualified. I promise them I am available at the last minute if they find no one else.

I end up having to keep my promise.

Why me? I am very uncomfortable and feel like crying at the conference—it's so quiet, and several people are blind, deaf, and in wheelchairs. How can they keep on? How to let them know how much I respect their courage and stamina, how to get over my awe and the moat that my awe digs between us?

And so, after a lot of practice, I begin my talk, using sign language. Nervously I make my opening remarks, signing (I later find out), "I'm so pregnant to be with you today . . . "

Heartened by the deep listening of my deaf audience and assisted by my signer, I tell them how much I've wanted to avoid the constant calls and voice mails from Patty O'Sullivan, their organizer; how I know ev-

Radical Stand

BE THE CHANGE
YOU WANT
TO SEE

ery time she calls there will be one more thing for me to do. And I urge them to keep it up, to stay in the face of people like me who don't have time for them, to keep it up until things change and they get everything—everything—they need and deserve.

I walk away inspired by their forgiveness, courage, and persistence and deeply grateful that I work in a corporate culture where it is not okay not to respect each other.

A week later, Patty waltzes into my office with a gold plaque, which she proudly bestows upon me, assuring me I am the first to receive this award. The plaque is engraved with the hand sign for "Thank you." Below it is inscribed, "Thank You for 'In Your Face.'"

So-Called Budget Reform

Later that year, one midnight as I'm doing e-mail, my fussy boy finally asleep, I blink three times as my adrenaline begins to pump: I can't believe what I'm reading. It seems HP is supporting California Governor Wilson's 1993 Budget Reform Initiative.

I know from my radical friends outside the company that "budget reform" is the euphemism for an initiative to reduce the Aid to Families with Dependent Children (AFDC) and other benefits going to the poorest women and children in the state.

Support for this initiative seems to me absolutely contrary to HP's citizenship objective and I am really upset. How can we be good citizens—we, the wealthiest in our communities—if we support cutting benefits for the poorest?

At the same time, I'm tired, with already too much to

do. Can I really do anything that will matter when The Company has decided to go this route? I, as one employee?

I fade into thinking about my favorite movie—the way I choose to remember it . . .

In "The Year of Living Dangerously," a journalist in '60s Indonesia is covering the downfall of the Sukarno government. He hangs around with the rest of the journalists, covering the same things they are, until he meets a nondescript "little man" played by Linda Hunt. Before long, this little man has gotten the journalist into the most important government parties, into the heart of the guerilla movement, to the girlfriend of his dreams, and so on.

Then the journalist stumbles into the little man's digs one afternoon to discover on the man's desk an entire folder about himself, with the equivalent of a job description, performance review, and development plan. The journalist is enraged and demands that the little man tell him who he is. As I recall it, the journalist cries out, "Who do you think you are to have files on me?" And the little man replies, "Who got you all your best contacts with the government, the opposition, even your girlfriend? I am who I am. . . . "

The lesson I take from this is that being marginal can be very powerful. The little man is unimportant—he looks like a servant—so he can get into any society party or top government meeting he wants. He looks like a peasant, so the guerrillas trust him. He isn't sexually appealing, so he threatens neither women nor men, and can act as the matchmaker. Being non-technical in a high-tech company and in Personnel to boot is being fairly marginal, and relative to the line-management jobs, it's not threatening. Line managers blow us off all the time. The more marginal one is, the more one can speak truth to the powers that be with impunity.

The medieval courts had their fools to round out the king's picture of reality. The contemporary corporation has me and others like me . . .

Radical Move

TAP THE
STRENGTH
OF YOUR
RELATIONSHIPS

I come back to the phone in my hand and send voice mails to fifteen people who I think would feel the same way about this, or who might have some information to bear. "Did you read this?" I ask. "What do you know about it? What does it mean? My first reaction is that it's very disappointing and in misalignment with our values as a company. What do you think?"

I get lots of responses with information, elaboration, and similar sentiments. Where once there was only my voice, I have amplified it and there are now fifteen of us. This gives me the information and the platform and the confidence to keep going.

Then I go outside the company to amplify my own voice. I talk to activist friends and people at other companies, and I confirm that this is indeed a big thing.

Groups like the local Council of Churches and children's advocacy groups, including one headed by the former president of Stanford, are saying this is a terrible thing.

Now I have a choice. I can assume that HP is the corporate bad guy my radical friends (and some part of me) think it is, or I can assume that top management must not know about this aspect of the budget reform bill. I decide on the latter. I decide to assume that HP is decent and fair, just ill-informed. I assume the company wants to do the right thing.

From that stance, I can act. My next step is to contact our CEO. Do I know John Young? Not really. Our paths did cross at a recent HP Labs meeting, though, so I decide to make another positive assumption. I assume we have a relationship and approach him from that point of view.

I send John an e-mail thanking him for his great comments at that meeting, then I add that I was quite alarmed to read that HP is supporting the Budget Reform Initiative. I summarize my research. I mention the full-page newspaper ad that's just appeared, headlined "Why Are California's Richest Citizens Conspiring to Rob Its Poorest Citizens?" The ad goes on to compare the salary of the CEO of a Bay Area company to the monthly chit of a welfare mother. I let him know what I've learned: that this ad is just the first of many that are planned. Each week will feature a different CEO. His own name and salary are already in the lineup. I remind him that it's the local Council of Churches and the local labor unions who are paying for the ads.

I tell him that the former president of Bill and Dave's alma mater, Stanford University, has called the budget reform "unspeakably cruel to children." I add that the children who will not be eating breakfast have names for me—my own kids' friends figure among the children at risk.

I ask if there isn't some alternative—perhaps a legislative solution for balancing the budget that would leave AFDC alone? (I know there is, I know we've even considered it, but chose instead to support the governor.)

Our CEO e-mails a response within twenty-four hours,

shares his own misgivings about the company position, and tells me he's asked our head of Government Affairs to explore alternatives. Later I learn from friends close to the decision that my e-mail to John has catalyzed a reversal of our support, and we are throwing all our resources behind the legislative solution, which would leave AFDC intact.

Radical Tool

TURN "ENEMIES"
INTO ALLIES

I find myself thinking how my understanding of "the company" and "corporate" has changed since I've worked at HP. "The corporation" is not the homogeneous, nefarious, unyielding monster I once thought. It's an aggregation of people who make decisions, sometimes bad ones. And, we can—and will—change these decisions if the disadvantages outweigh the advantages, and if people are around to point out that fact or make it a fact.

In the end, the 1993 Budget Reform Initiative dies for lack of support.

White, Loving Someone Black

I don't know what it is to grow up black in this country, but I know what it is to love someone who is—and it's the most joy and also the most pain I have ever known. Meeting my children's birth mothers, coming to love them and share the pain of their broken dreams and relentlessly cruel worlds, I walk through the invisible veil that until then has separated me from the true devastation of poverty and racism in America. After each adoption I get physically very sick. And I am haunted by the question How can I make a difference?

I am watching the lights go out in my daughter's sparkling eyes during the preschool years. We can't figure it out.
Her teachers are good, the schools are recommended. Yet this
child, so lively at home, clams up and gets catatonic in the
classroom. Even though they ask almost
nothing of her, she seems scared. What is
going on?

Radical Move

RECRUIT CO-
CONSPIRATORS

We talk to parents of other adopted and
black children, and soon have a support
group going. We uncover powerful, limiting
assumptions people have about our children,
assumptions that will later help us under-
stand, as well, the rage our son develops in his preschool
years. These are:

- Adopted black children are drug babies and therefore brain damaged. Don't expect anything of them.
- For the same offense, big black boys are "evil," little
  white boys are "naughty." (This was pointed out by
  a white parent comparing the way her son and his
  black friend are treated.)
- Boys and girls of *any* color who won't sit on a carpet
  square and listen to a story for half an hour should
  be medicated. Fifteen minutes of recess is sufficient
  for an active, growing child; any hyperactivity after
  the fifteen minutes of exercise is proof they need
  meds.
- There are no black boys, really. There are only black
  men, just little. They will grow up to become rap-
  ists and murderers and should be punished now

while we've got them. "We've got to teach them a lesson while we still can," as one teacher told a parent in our group whose son is black.

- Kids are dangerous. (In the experience of our group, some of the parents of our kids' friends—the parents who are virulently prejudiced, especially those who are unconscious about it—are far more dangerous to our children than the other children.)

We move our children often, in search of placements that are sensitive to these hidden assumptions. We find support at all levels in the system, from principals who risk their jobs to switch our placements, to an African American teacher who accompanies us to a hearing, to a Caucasian teacher who dreams our son's dreams.

And over the years, we develop an African American extended family that includes a dad, three uncles, a grandmother, four aunts, and numerous cousins. This is the safety net that catches us when we're falling, reminds us of worse situations over which people have triumphed, puts us in touch with the hidden network of African American and other ethnicities that "get it," and steps in to make the difference that literally saves us.

Practicing Witchcraft

It's 1996 and I am at a wonderful regional Technical Women's Conference in Boise, Idaho. Among other things, the keynote speaker, Executive Vice President Dick Hackborn, tells us, "As the metrics for gauging success in our businesses become 'hard' measures and less a matter of subjective opinion, women and minorities will excel. When the question is, 'Did you get the sale or not?' or 'Did you exceed quota or not?' you will rise to the highest levels. This is already happening in my own part of the company, where shrinking margins and a faster pace have produced harder metrics. Let's face it, you had to be twice as smart as the white men to get hired in the first place." He gets a standing ovation.

My friend Bonnie Severy and I lead what turns out to be an amazing workshop. We had thought it would attract twenty or so—and it gets four hundred attendees! At the last minute, we're changing rooms and getting made up for the big-screen TV.

Leveraging Catherine Bateson's wonderful book *Composing a Life*, our workshop, "Quest vs. Quilt: Composing a Work Life," resonates with a lot of women. I share my tears upon reading the first chapter in the book, tears of relief that for once, I see how my life makes sense. I share my resumé from hell, the one I am always having to edit and leave things out of so it looks like a "quest" resume. ("Yes, all my life everything I have ever done has led to my being a personnel manager!" Right.)

In fact, my work life is not a quest but a quilt of many-textured colorful shapes, which somehow make up the unique and colorful me. I am grateful for that quilt; its patches are the memories in which I wrap myself when times are cold.

Bonnie and I share other books we've read and found helpful, and some of the tools: meditation, incense, the *I Ching*, tarot, crystals. All these things evoke the wisdom in the right brain, so difficult to access in our left-lobe, linear, hyper-analytic culture. I remark that I keep crystals and several tarot decks on my desk in the personnel office, with a standing invitation for people to borrow them, and they frequently disappear for a time, only to return with gifts. A week after the workshop I get a phone call from the conference planner. Sounding scared, she says that one of our workshop participants went home very upset. Her husband has written a letter to the vice president heading her part of HP—and cc'd everybody in between—saying that there is a personnel manager in HP promoting occultism and witchcraft, and what would *Fortune* magazine do with this if they found out? The woman calling me wonders if I would be willing to talk to this irate husband?

I say, "Of course," because that is what you say at HP.

I alternate between fear and rage as I try to reach this man. Fear that I could lose my job, or just as bad, my credibility in my job. Rage that this woman goes home from a women's conference and gets her husband to fight her battles, and now I have to deal with someone who wasn't even there!

Fortunately, despite many attempts, I do not reach the husband for several days. In the meantime, a little voice tells me to calm down and remember the religion of my Southern childhood. How frightened I had been—of everything, because it all seemed to be of the devil, with enormous power to pull me off track. My fear for my friends was so great that I actually converted my best friend, whose parents were devout believers in a completely different tradition, to my faith.

When I finally reach the husband, I am feeling sad. Sad that I've somehow frightened him and his wife. I tell him this and explain what we were trying to do: help people access their full intelligence. We talk a little about his faith. I share that I went to divinity school, have a degree in theology, and worked with the churches for over a decade. I quote passages from his tradition that exemplify the use of both sides of the brain.

Radical Move

START A
CONVERSATION—
AND LISTEN!

Radical Tool

TURN "ENEMIES"
INTO ALLIES

He is much calmer by now, but wonders why I have listed no books from his tradition on my bibliography. I'm surprised, actually, that I haven't, as there are books in mystical traditions within his own faith. I promise to amend the bibliography and invite him to do the next workshop with me, as by this point in the conversation, it seems that together we could do something that would work for everyone. He laughs, declines the invitation, and we part friends.

Two days later, I am awestruck when I am cc'd on a letter he has written to the same vice president—and everybody in between—saying he had not attended the workshop and had not understood my intentions. Having had a conversation with me, he now understands my intentions and supports them.

Chapter 4

THE COURAGE TO LISTEN

Conversation is both the medium and the message of the information economy. We are knowledge workers. We are not so much doing things to "stuff" anymore—manufacturing things or processing raw materials—we are having conversations and generating new ideas. We are talking to each other and listening each other into speech.

i

It's 1993, three years since I started the personnel manager job here at HP Labs—and I'm ready do something more. Something bigger, with greater impact, something systemic. But what?

The thing is, HP Labs is doing well: developing and transferring a record number of new technologies to HP's different business units, which turn them into customer products. What's more, these are high-impact technologies, inventions that can start a new business or significantly extend an existing business.

Thanks to our technology transfer rate, we are getting 12 to 15 percent funding increases every year while other central R&D organizations are downsizing or shutting down. *Fortune* magazine features us as the Mecca where other labs come to learn how we maintain our relatively high transfer rate. We have no burning platform, no reason to jump into the icy, violent seas of change and drown or start swimming.

So we're doing well, but as three technology centers, as

twelve independent technology labs within those centers, and even as individual engineers, we're like silos. We all function separately, with little synergy between parts and a lid on top of each. As personnel manager I ask myself, "What could make a difference here?" I don't know. But what I do know is that operating in this mode, we will never achieve our new director's vision of "MC^2": a future for the company where its unique combination of strengths—measurement, communication, and computers—would be *integrated* to create solutions that will open up markets for us that are inaccessible to companies with only one or two of these strengths. MC^2 connotes for us the energy and ingenuity that could be released by this integration of technologies—something that could be explosively creative for HP.

I share my frustrations with our new director, my manager, Joel Birnbaum, the senior vice president of R&D for HP. He responds with a question he's had for fifteen years: "Why does no one out there consider HP Labs the best industrial research lab in the world?" He suggests I check with consulting firms to see if we can get some help.

I interview several top firms, telling them we want to become the world's best industrial research lab. I am frustrated with the generic solutions they offer and horrified at the costs, both financial and in terms of disruptions to our ongoing work. They want $300,000 for a needs assessment, $1 million a year for at least three years, and up to ten consultants at a time living with us! And this is supposed to be a good thing? Am I missing something here? I ask my friend Sara Beckman, an HP internal consultant, to interview the most prestigious of my rejects to see if I'm just out of date:

Her Ph.D. is much newer than mine and she's currently on the faculty at Berkeley and MIT while I'm in the trenches. She does the interviews and confirms my judgment.

Shortly after I ask myself this question, the *Wall Street Journal* runs an article on big consulting firms and notes, "The increasingly complex and technology-driven marketplace doesn't make things easier for generalist advisors." According to one dissatisfied customer, "Their work is canned, their formats are canned, their thinking is canned, and they give black-box solutions to everything, where every situation is unique."

I share my findings with Joel. "This is what I'm getting from the consulting firms and I don't think they're going to help. We're still going to have to do all the work, so why don't we just get to it?" He says, "Okay then, you lead the effort. You have a Ph.D. You must know something about this. Replace yourself as personnel manager and do this full time."

I break into a cold sweat and confess, "Joel, I know using a big consulting firm won't work, but that doesn't mean I know what *will* work."

"Well, that's a good start," he responds. "Think about the job and get back to me."

Radical Stand

PUT A STAKE IN
THE GROUND

Suddenly, over the next few days, stronger than I've ever felt it since I joined HP, I remember why I came here a decade ago. After years working to change the world through politics, education, government, and the churches, I believe I can have more impact through the corporate sector because more than any other sector, it will determine the future of the world.

I've made some difference at and through HP, and now I

dream again: vivid, electrifying, wake-up-in-the-middle-of-the-night kinds of dreams, of HP raising the bar for global companies, redefining corporate citizenship to include not just the twenty-mile radius around our factories, but the world as our neighborhood. What if this is a way to get started? Feeling terrified, because I have no idea even how to begin, I tell Joel, "I'm on!"

Admitting We Don't Know

I ask Joel if he'll share his question about being the "world's best" in his upcoming employee coffee talks around the world. He hesitates. "How can I do that? I don't even know what I mean by 'best'! Most number of patents? Most Nobel laureates or fellows of the Institute of Electrical and Electronics Engineers? Highest rate of technology transfers? A clearly focused research agenda? Ability to recognize the most critical projects and consistently focus resources on them? Ability to stop work that doesn't matter? Or does it even matter if we're 'the best'?"

I persist. "Well, why don't we just ask? I mean, wouldn't it be something for you to stand up there with the question and invite everyone to respond with their own questions and answers? We have to do our annual HP employee survey starting in a few weeks; why not make it work for this? We'll add our own questions. We'll ask people what they think 'world's best' is and what we need to do to get there. Save ourselves $300,000. Why not?"

Now, you have to remember that this is the man who correctly convinced a very skeptical company to bet on RISC (Reduced Instruction Set Computing) technology, a radical new computer architecture. He is where he is today because he has the answers. How will it go down when this respected leader starts to talk about not knowing what he's talking about? On the other hand, this is not your run-of-the-mill guy: He's married to a Metropolitan Opera singer and quotes Shelley

Radical Stand

BE WILLING NOT
TO KNOW

and Goethe to explain his points. He's not afraid of poetry, passion, or ambiguity. Somehow this seems promising.

Joel says yes, and over the next five months, he shares his vision questions at HP Labs sites around the world, asking each employee, "What do you think?" and requesting their response in the employee survey. He announces he's promoted me to work full time on the "World's Best Industrial Research Labs" (WBIRL) project and given me a $250,000 budget. We add four specific questions to the 1993 Employee Survey:

1. What would it take to become world's best?
2. Why aren't we?
3. Is what you are working on world class? If not, why not?
4. What do you need to be your best?

Radical Move

RECRUIT CO-
CONSPIRATORS,
START A
CONVERSATION—
AND LISTEN!

Looking back, I can see the critical characteristics of Joel's vision of HP Labs as the "world's best." Instead of declaring a vision, as leaders are exhorted to do by consultants and executive coaches and all the how-to management books, Joel asks vision questions, catalyzing an organization-wide vision inquiry, inviting the collaboration of all, as equal voices, in creating our vision.

What a relief not to have something shoved down our throats from above!

Instead of a one-way broadcast, he launches an organization-wide web of communication and dialogue; he asks the employees what the WBIRL questions mean for their own jobs, giving them a way to immediately respond, individually. By asking each employee what the questions mean to him or her, Joel transforms high-level management rhetoric into individual personal responsibility.

And by asking whether we should even be asking the question, Joel creates a context where even nonparticipation and resistance are valid forms of participation. I marvel at his brilliance.

And his courage. He takes the risk, sharing a dream he can't define and questions to which he has no answers.

By using the employee survey for the needs assessment rather than developing and using a new tool, we set the stage for a practice throughout the coming years that we name "lite touch" and that, several years later, Ed Gurowitz of the Generative Leadership Group will clarify for me as "minimalism." I call it "tweak, don't toss." It means: Perturb the system as little as possible to accomplish your goal.

Radical Tool

TWEAK,
DON'T TOSS

• Don't introduce something new if you can use something old to accomplish your purpose.
• Use what's at hand, begin now, to get

the ball rolling. Worry about progress, not perfection.

- Replace "How?" with "Do!" Take action. It will create momentum, and set things and people in motion. Just get started and see what happens. You can always make midcourse corrections if you need to.

- Ask people everywhere what they see. In the aggregate all the people have a better picture of the whole system than any expert inside or outside the organization can provide.

- Help people do what they want to do that's right in front of them. Senior management works on what they see for themselves to do. The newest employee does the same. In the aggregate, the small, incremental changes add up to an organizational transformation. There's no need to "cascade" change from the top, as if there's an empty receptacle at the bottom just waiting to be filled.

When the employee surveys come in, we get eight hundred pages of feedback, single spaced. The computer center that analyzes these things cannot deal with it. I take it home, curl up on the couch, and read page after page of frustration, dreams, and insights. Then, using an inductive approach, I cluster the themes I see, then cluster the clusters until I build up to a high-level view of what we, in the aggregate, think about why we're not the world's best lab and what it would take to become the best.

There seem to be three areas of concern:

- Programs: Too many projects, no strategic priorities; everything underresourced.

- People: Poor performers are not removed soon enough or at all; we're not attracting or retaining top researchers; employees aren't trusted to sign for even small purchases required to do their jobs; support employees are second class; the work environment is less supportive of women and minorities than of majority men.
- Processes: Information-technology infrastructure—design tools, computer and workstation support and access—is not even as good as that in some of our manufacturing divisions. And our engineers are supposed to be working three to five years out. Forget the WBIRL! HP Labs, alone among HP divisions, has no Quality program.

I create a set of overhead slides about the survey results for the senior managers, and then realize *this isn't it!* Eight hundred pages of frustration, dreams, and insights reduced to bullets and pie charts of issues that senior management is supposed to fix? And the embedded paradigm of helpless employees and omniscient managers is absurd.

Is there a way to bring the employees' voices into the room where I will present the report to HP Labs management? And suggest that a collective "we" go to work on this instead of "us" (management) fixing "them" (the employees)?

Bringing in the Missing Voices

I dread the idea that is dawning for me: to use a technique I learned in political street theater and in the women's movement. It's called Readers' Theater and I dread it because

I'm still afraid when my radical roots seem to offer the best solutions. I mean, the last time I did Readers' Theater, I wore combat boots and had a shaved head. One of these days, I'm going to get busted. Maybe today is the day. Can I really bring "the streets" and these "radical" techniques into the corporate world?

In Readers' Theater, several people read their own or other people's stories on a certain topic or issue. Its purpose is to raise consciousness, to hold up a mirror that will make the whole visible to the parts and let the whole system begin to see the emotion, the passion behind the observations we usually just put into bullet points on overhead slides. Flattened out into numbers on plastic, people's pain, perceptions, and insights are lost. The soul of the people is missing.

Radical Tool

HOLD UP A
MIRROR

I run my idea by Sharon Connor, my friend who replaced me as personnel manager when I started the "world's best" full time. She's got better judgment than I do about what can fly below the radar and I consult her often. What does she think? She says, "Go for it! See what it looks like, and then decide!" I decide to go with the idea. Readers' Theater is exactly what we need to do so that senior managers "get" what the whole body of HP Labs employees says stands in the way of our being "best" in the world and what we need to do to change.

I select quotes from the survey that represent the major points and suggested solutions in the three areas of concern we uncovered and show the passion and character of our folks, and I weave them into a "play" about HP Labs. Then I recruit six managers to act out the thoughts and feelings of the engineers and secretaries, and six engineers and secretaries to act out the managers' thoughts and feelings. Each part represents a job function. It goes like this:

A SENIOR ENGINEER: "The problem is we're not getting the best students from the best schools."

AN ENTRY-LEVEL ENGINEER: "I've been here two months and my computer still doesn't work."

A SECRETARY: "The problem is Finance and Personnel are downsizing and dumping all of the work on the admin."

A SENIOR MANAGER: "The problem is I'm supposed to be customer-facing—dealing with the divisions we'll transfer our new technologies to *and* with the end-user customers those technologies are designed for. How do I have time to manage and support my people?"

A TECHNICIAN: "The problem is there's no Management by Wandering Around. I haven't even met my lab director."

ANOTHER SENIOR ENGINEER: "The best in the world? The 'best' central research lab is the one that has the best marketing department and can get the best public relations."

At the end of the "play," the thirty senior managers are very quiet. Then they start clapping. Then there's a long silence. We take a break. Then the excitement starts to show: "I really got it," "I really see what is going on in HP Labs now." One of the brilliant senior scientists on the management team declares, "This theater is the only way these data can convey the information."

While senior managers usually delegate the response to

the employee survey to the local managers closer to the issues, this year, in response to the play, they also develop the first ever HP Labs-level plan reflecting their own commitments to address the issues of strategic priority setting, people management, and the work environment. They dub this plan "Hoshin-Lite," because it does not operate like the typical Hoshin. A traditional Hoshin is a plan that originates at the top and cascades down to the lowest member in the hierarchy. When the entire Hoshin is complete, the plan for each level supports the objective of the level *above* it, and is the context for the plan of the level *below* it. The problem with this is that all the thinking comes from the top.

The Hoshin-Lite that these senior managers create is the only management plan in the company that doesn't cascade down through the organization. They are making themselves responsible for achieving their own plan, and are modeling for each level below to do the same.

The senior-management plan has two parts. They are going to benchmark output metrics, to see how other central research labs measure themselves. They are also going to look at how to allocate resources so that there is enough flexibility to staff the serendipitous things that come along while at the same time using resources well throughout the year. Their Hoshin-Lite begins and ends with them. They share it in their own employee coffee talks, and invite employees to work on whatever problems *they* think will make a difference from their own perspective. Their plan doesn't have to be a subset of the next-higher-level's plan. In my mind, Hoshin is a mechanical model; it works top down. The person at the top of the hierarchy knows the most, so here are your orders—march! Hoshin-Lite is a living systems model, allowing to each part of the organization its own intelligence and priorities in the service of the good of the whole.

Looking back, making the whole of the system visible to the parts becomes an ongoing intervention at individual and organizational levels. In the presence of the whole, people seem to understand themselves as the "missing piece." They see what they need to do and the difference they can make. In this case, through Readers' Theater, the entire organization shows up in the room and becomes the context for senior managers to create their first-ever joint plan—and with unprecedented focus and urgency.

I have a budget of $250,000 set aside to get started with a big consulting company. Instead, with Joel's full support, I send out an e-mail to our employees telling them the money is for them. I ask them to check in with me if they need any of it to realize their dreams for our becoming world's best. This turns out to be a really good move for me as their supposed change guru—my title is now "Worldwide Change Manager"—because I don't know what help they need. I turn nobody down who bids for a piece of that first $250,000, no matter what they want it for. But most don't even want money. They just want to be listened to and appreciated.

Managing Change

Which is just as well. How does a "change manager" manage change anyway? The whole concept is new. But as news of my new title makes its way through the tendrils of the company grapevine, I start hearing from others who are saddled or honored (depending on what day you talk to them) with the same designation, or who want just such a job.

Six of us change managers decide to meet and compare notes. We end up developing a Readers' Theater presentation for an upcoming Technical Women's Conference that will not only hold up a mirror to help each of us see what the others are doing, but will scale up and become the window on what we're doing so everyone else can see it too.

Radical Tool

HOLD UP A MIRROR

As we write our script, what we discover is a growing—though unofficial—recognition across HP that when revolutionary changes are called for, someone needs to create and manage the process. This is pretty much where our similarities end.

We come from personnel, marketing, manufacturing, quality, and engineering. We range from executives to entry-level people. We have different philosophies on how to support our organization or department's large-scale changes.

Of course, the six of us immediately get into who's right and who's wrong and what the best approach is—grassroots, top-down, formal, informal. But after a lot of back and forth, we realize "right" or "wrong" is really not the issue. The issue is, what's possible in your setting given who you are, who your management is, and what's needed—and based on those realities, use the approach that will work best. While I prefer grassroots leadership but am willing to use the formal, top-down approach (planning sessions, senior-management offsites) when I need to, others take just the opposite approach.

I regard "change manager" as an oxymoron, like "jumbo shrimp" or "airplane food." I think you can create the conditions for change to *emerge*, but if you "manage" it, you kill it. Some of my colleagues, who align more with the top-down approach, believe it describes well what they do.

Our objectives as change managers are quite different, too. One woman is revamping the whole Test and Measurement Organization from being a hardware business to becoming a systems business that incorporates software along with the traditional products. Another is working on the re-invention of Corporate Training, co-creating with her executive customers just-in-time consulting, training, and development for every stage in the value chain leading to revenue.

Radical Move

RECRUIT
CO-CONSPIRATORS

Finding co-conspirators in this new work boosts the confidence and skills of each of us, and gives those who want to become change managers the language, conceptual frameworks, business justification, and tools to create these jobs that accelerate and improve the change process throughout the company.

Year One: The Floodgates Open

Among the many people I talk with that first year of the WBIRL program, 1994, there are some who don't buy what I'm up to. Several senior managers candidly state, "We don't need this program; we shouldn't be wasting your head count and $250,000 on it." At first, I am threatened. I really want this job. Then I ask myself, "What if they are right? What's the truth here?"

One of these managers is Technology Center Director Ed Karrer. I can always count on him to tell me the truth straight to my face, and to answer all my questions. Ed believes that WBIRL could be very helpful for support functions (like admin, personnel, and finance) and for improvements in the research process but not for improving the quality of the research content itself. He's had the experience of consultants coming in and slowing down the work.

Radical Stand

USE OBSTACLES AS INFORMATION

So together we explore what Quality programs could do for the support functions. And Ed becomes my best partner going forward. Thanks to just these qualities of minimalism, truth telling, and the willingness to answer all my questions and partner with me, Ed and I—who come from opposite ends of the spectrum on most problems—forge a robust path together.

Radical Tool

TURN "ENEMIES" INTO ALLIES

Ironically, just as I abandon any work on the research agenda, senior management itself begins in this very first year to use the WBIRL framework and budget to focus the research agenda. Even so, in deference to their initial objections, I take the opening they've given me for a Quality program and reframe additional projects in year one as our new Quality effort focused on support activities.

Besides these senior managers, others call me with their ideas. Almost always they wonder if they are wasting my time. They come from all levels, job functions, and geographies, sharing their insights, frustrations, and dreams.

Whenever anybody comes to talk to me about an idea and stumblingly gets it out, I say, "Great idea." Automatically. No matter what the idea is. I believe it is not my job to judge, but to reward their courage and passion and willingness to put a stake in the ground with whatever help I can offer. And I make a discovery. Whenever I suspend judgment and say, "Great idea," I find myself beginning to think how it might actually *be* a great idea, even if the judgment machine in the back of my mind is going, "Oh, jeez. I can't believe this. It'll never work."

Radical Tool

PLAY WITH
WHOEVER
SHOWS UP

So I encourage the idea, I ask questions, I listen, and we start thinking about how we can make it happen. We explore the connections between their ideas and others' similar or complementary ideas. Then we imagine the biggest impact their efforts can make. Sometimes they need money from my grants budget—for everything from consultants to travel, classes, and equipment—but mostly they just need validation.

Radical Move

RECRUIT
CO-CONSPIRATORS,
START A
CONVERSATION—
AND LISTEN!

The principle underlying the grants program is minimalism again. Tweak, don't toss. Don't go too far out and don't do very much. So the grants program just sits there, inviting people to come to it. It doesn't tell them, "We're going to do X," and it isn't a request for proposals, saying, "In this area we're going to fund Y." We just announce it and see what shows up.

Radical Tool

TWEAK,
DON'T TOSS

At the end of the first year, I prepare a progress report for WBIRL. I inventory work groups, discovering some I didn't even know about. In one year, thirty-six work groups have sprung up, involving over one-third of HP Labs' twelve hundred people from all levels of the organization! (And only half of them needed grant money.) The lid is off and all questions are fair game!

For example:

- "What should our business fundamentals be as support functions to the researchers?" asks Ian Osborne, the Bristol operations manager—and so launches HP Labs' Quality program.

- "How can we improve the quality of our work lives and our contribution to HP Labs?" ask secretaries Nancy Freeze, Carole Gize, Sharon Hanrahan, and Gail Wakelee—and create the first sitewide Secretaries Forum. In just a year, the forum rewrites the corporate shipping manual for the entire company and reduces from thirteen to one the number of forms required to enroll a new employee. These two projects alone save HP thousands of hours of bureaucracy and red tape and hundreds of thousands of dollars. The Secretaries Forum also launches an ongoing self-development seminar program. By the second year, the secretary who wants to be promoted out of the function gets her wish, and the Forum continues to thrive.

- "Why don't we talk to each other, even at the coffee pots?" ask Chandrakant Patel and Prasad Raje, two gregarious engineers—and start the Friday afternoon "chalk talks" to toss around whatever technological issues people are grappling with. In their first two years, the chalk talks draw anywhere from 15 to 150 engineers; in their third year they become a regular sponsored part of the HP Labs program.

In that third year, having handed off the local program, Chandrakant decides to scale up and hold an HP-wide chalk talk on his technology obsession: how to keep our chips and systems cool. He passionately feels this is an issue that gets very little visibility throughout HP and realizes that, in order for HP to be competitive with our "always on" architecture, we have to develop a portfolio of cooling solutions for the future. He has already put his stake in the ground about this issue. But he is a lone voice, crying in the wilderness, and only an engineer. He recruits a co-conspirator, Christian Belady of High Performance Systems Division, who's based in Texas. Together, they reserve a large conference room and invite five other people in the company they know who talk about cooling—and ninety people show up for two days!

Radical Tool

SCALE UP

Radical Move

RECRUIT
CO-CONSPIRATORS,
BUILD YOUR
CADRE

This no-budget conference serves to amplify the positive deviance of the token few, scattered among 120,000 employees, who care about this issue and launches a conversation and community that now pervades the company. The fourth annual conference is held in HP Roseville in late 2000. And weekly, the "COOL TEAM" of one hundred engineers, technicians, and managers around the company meet by phone, e-mail, and conference call to cool our servers, PCs, and computers. Through the technology developed out of this conversation, this team delivers tens of millions of dollars to the bottom line, and with regard to cooling, leaves our competitors far behind.

Radical Tool

AMPLIFY
POSITIVE DEVIANCE

- "How can we get mentored?" asks a group of newer engineers—and with five thousand dollars from my budget for an in-house consultant, they create the HP Labs Mentoring Program. By the end of three years, it has helped develop more than thirty pairs of new engineers and manager-mentors.

- "What do our customers—both internal and external—expect from us," ask the senior managers, "and how are those expectations changing?" Interviews reveal a new role for HP Labs and a new foundation for our output metrics. The new role? The vice presidents of HP's business sectors expect HP Labs to help lead the company in creating new businesses, in addition to our more traditional role of developing technologies to expand upon the current businesses.

Moving into this new role, we initiate multidisciplinary strategic initiatives, and over the next few years we will start business-development task forces in areas as diverse as health care and home electronics; rapid prototyping—including user trials; visiting senior technical contributors in critical emergent technologies; expanded global external research; and new initiatives in basic research into nonlinear algorithms and molecular computing.

• "How do we measure the output of a central research lab?" Ed Karrer, the director of our Measurement Research Center, and Ian Osborne, the operations manager of our Bristol lab, analyze the interview data and new benchmarking data to produce our output metrics. We will now measure the output of HP Labs, each technology center, each technology lab, and each lab director in three ways, in this priority.

The first metric is financial—the bottom-line value of technologies transferred, measured by how many new businesses or extensions resulted from these technologies, and the significance of the businesses to the bottom line. The second metric is customer satisfaction—as measured by division and executive feedback. Interestingly, this metric is second by choice of the very customers advising us. They recognize that there are critical times when we should not listen to them, and we should not be penalized if they're unhappy with us at those times. Here's why: If this metric were first and took priority over financial results, there would have been no ink jet, no RISC, no photonics.

The third metric, a distant third—and this is a shock to some of our top technical people—is scientific contribution. We are not a university research lab, but an industrial research lab. Even the most exciting inventions and discoveries will not be valued highly if they can't be commercialized. Within a year, these metrics are adopted across the organization.

- "How do other world-class central research labs allocate their resources to provide the flexibility for opportunistic projects and at the same time provide for multiyear funding?" asks Andrew Liu, the division controller—who then launches worldwide benchmarking. Despite being resisted at first, his team recommends changes throughout the research agenda's strategic decision-making process. Three major changes further the Labs' new role of creating new businesses, based on MC^2, Joel Birnbaum's vision for capitalizing on the integration of HP's expertise in measurement, communication, and computers.

First, Andrew's team recommends that we reserve incremental growth in our budget for the serendipitous and for new priorities. Second, they call for an end to the tradition that the measurement and analysis labs present their annual plans for new technologies to the measurement and analytic businesses, while computing presents to the computing side of the company. Instead, they recommend that the entire portfolio of HP Labs be tailored for each of the major businesses—so that each part of the company gets a tailored preview of new work, new opportunities, and potential new businesses in all three of our MC^2 areas of expertise. Third, they recommend in-depth reviews of each technology center by the other centers in HP Labs. When implemented, these last two recommendations put windows on all the silos and create conditions that result in a surge of MC^2 cross-center and cross-lab collaborations leading to new business creation.

- "How can HP Labs make better strategic decisions?" Technology-center director Dick Lampman takes the lead to address this critical question. This project is complex and gets to the heart of the research agenda. Traditionally, each technology center is a silo that gets growth money to develop technologies for extending its silo business. In the course of considering this question for their annual meeting, Dick's team realizes that the biggest opportunities are cross-silo, and they will be driven by the company's choices about its future. We must know HP Labs' next-larger context: HP's future. We query HP senior management for their visions of the future and learn they are expecting these visions from us. We must imagine and invent alternative futures for HP. Then we will know how to invest our R&D dollars.

- "What's the ideal turnover rate for HP Labs' portfolio?" Ed Karrer takes the lead and starts by identifying the current project lifetime as five years, on average. At this rate, 20 percent of HP Labs projects should be killed each year, and soon our strategic offsites will require each center director to identify the 20 percent that have to go. At first, this is an agonizing process, but as it frees up resources for new opportunities, a positive feedback loop emerges that makes this process more palatable. The trick, of course, is that you don't necessarily get to keep the 20 percent you free up, as another center may have more strategic uses for the resource.

Finding a Keynote Listener

In keeping with "world's best," Joel's senior staff wants a great keynote speaker for our annual strategic-management off-site where we will develop visions for the future. I ask Joel (I think the others will reject the idea out of hand), "What if instead of a great speaker, we have a great listener who can 'hear the managers into speech' about their visions for HP's future driven by the integration of HP Labs' technologies?"

Joel listens me into a halting extrapolation of this idea, as I draw on radical feminist theology and the pedagogies of women's consciousness-raising. He expresses his skepticism but with a wry smile encourages me to work on the idea. He offers me a coveted half hour at his staff meeting to make a proposal for a keynote listener that his staff can't refuse.

I first heard about the generative power of listening from Nelle Morton, the late feminist theologian and author of *The Journey Is Home,* whom I knew during my years working with the church. She believed that listening is a great and powerful skill that opens the creative floodgates in the person being listened to. The listener's attentive, unbroken, and receptive silence invites the speaker to explore their thoughts and come up with ideas that they've never had before. Ideas that literally didn't exist, until they were "listened into speech."

I remember the bomb Nelle dropped into the theological world over three decades ago when she responded to theologians who, along with the Bible, assert that "In the beginning was the Word." She told them, "In the beginning was the Listening."

Nelle turned the conventional Western paradigm on its head, understanding that the listener is the active agent in the transaction, while the speaker is the one acted upon. Obviously, for the millions of women who have listened men into their speeches, seen them into their paintings, cheered them into their trophies, and appreciated them into their genius, she struck a chord.

I saw this in action among men early in my career at HP. One of my friends, whom I'll call Rob, was a brilliant, highly ranked engineer. In the next cubicle sat a friend I'll call Cal, a "performance problem," an engineer ranked marginally, who supposedly contributed nothing to the technical agenda. But the two were inseparable: Rob, standing before his white-board, marker in hand, gesturing and explaining as Cal mildly looked on, occasionally asking a question or two.

After several years, Rob left the company for a startup. I went to visit him and who do I see in his cubicle but Cal,

Radical Move

LISTEN SOMEONE
INTO SPEECH

looking on as Rob explains something. And I suddenly got it. Without Cal's listening, Rob is not only "speechless," but "thoughtless" as well. Rob needs Cal to listen to him so he can know what he is thinking, so he can think at all. Cal's role is absolutely vital, a full 50 percent of the creative process that resulted in what we called Rob's ideas. Yet Cal is considered a performance problem and Rob a brilliant scientist.

Okay. I know listening works, but oh, no! Readers' Theater, feminist theology, and now a listener as our keynote speaker? What is it about creating whole systems at the level of the organization that requires the whole of me? It's as if the change is a fractal that has to be embodied at every level of scale, beginning with the individual level, moving on to the HP Labs level, and even on to the company and global level of scale.

On the other hand, maybe I'm fooling myself. What if senior management's undoubted skepticism about a "keynote listener" turns out to be right?

Like Joel, I too doubt that the listener idea will be well received, but I accept his offer of a place on the agenda. Now I have to find a great keynote listener!

My partner in most of my "out of the box" schemes with Joel's staff is HP Labs' strategic-planning manager, Srinivas Suku-mar. Through the WBIRL project, I'm learning he is a man who deeply understands HP Labs' technologies and the future they could enable. He dreams of world peace, works daily on his own ego through meditation, and spends a month every year directing Gandhi peace camps for kids.

Radical Move

RECRUIT
CO-CONSPIRATORS,
TAP THE STRENGTH
OF YOUR
RELATIONSHIPS

Sukumar (who prefers to be called by his last name) is totally with me on my latest cockamamie idea. I call all my consultant friends, imploring them to come up with a "keynote listener" fast. My most generous, creative, out-of-the-box thought partner, Sandra Florstedt, a former HP employee, comes up with David Sibbet, an organizational consultant and graphic artist. She plops me into her car and drives me to San Francisco for an afternoon with him. He's the guy all right: a wonderful artist, bright technologist, deep listener, great facilitator, and, to top it off, a real mensch.

Sukumar and I and spend eight hours preparing David to be the "world's best" keynote listener, beginning with his half-hour irresistible proposal to Joel's staff, a bunch of brilliant skeptics. In fifteen minutes, David has these guys on the edge of their seats and is invited to the off-site, where he proceeds to "listen" these senior managers into the future.

As each manager speaks their vision, David listens deeply in order to draw "pictures" of these visions, so that the people speaking can "see what they mean." He uses the metaphor of a forest, which we decided on ahead of time. He understands the science behind the discussion and aggregates similar technologies (drawn as trees) into "groves." He sketches an aspen grove, where all the trees share a root system; a redwood grove, and more. He also organizes into an ecosystem those trees/technologies that enable others to live.

As the visual graphics begin to surround them, our senior staff sees evidence of their collaboration, connections they've never seen before, and the early prototypes of future businesses. What jump out are the core technologies that span alternative futures and must be invested in no matter which future the company pursues. For example, whether HP chooses to focus on building our medical, digital imaging, or telecommunications businesses, we will need to develop micromachining technologies. We will need competency in data compression—and to that end we will soon open a new lab in Israel.

Through this process it's also clear that the future lies in certain directions not dictated by the past. For example, we would better invest our measurement/analytic dollars in optical switching and biotechnology, away from gas chromatography and other medical projects. HP Labs' research agenda is getting clearer.

By the end of the day, in this large hotel room in Bristol, England, where the following week an upcoming *Masterpiece Theater* will be filmed, Joel's staff comes up with five specific and compelling visions for HP's future, each of which incorporates all three of our MC^2 competencies: measurement, communications, and computation—visions that we will soon prototype.

The automotive prototype inspires excitement but ultimately does not become a business because no single division is motivated to change enough to absorb it. The distributed measurement architecture affects many divisions and for this reason is hard to transfer to a single division for commercialization. Finally, though, it finds itself in virtually every product in our measurement, analytic, and medical businesses.

The medical-business prototypes all transfer, but with mixed success. Noninvasive biotechnical diagnostics becomes a robust business; the electronic medical record transfers with great excitement but ultimately fails to thrive; and at-home medical appliances transfer and, after a slow start, become viable.

The digital-photography vision presented at the off-site builds up through long years of effort combining expertise with color science, imaging, lens design, and signal processing. This program eventually transfers to the ink-jet printer organization, which commercializes it into a breakthrough new camera, scanners, and other new image products. This program also lays the groundwork for later image-related Internet services.

The information-utility vision eventually becomes the basis for HP's future in e-services. A decade before this off-site, Joel envisioned a utility delivering bit streams just like electric utilities deliver power. At this off-site, his vision gains momentum and eventually develops into a novel Internet-based middleware that will become "E-Speak," an open-source product that, combined with information appliances developed in HP Labs, becomes a key component of the company's e-services offerings in 2000.

Despite many attempts over the next five years, HP Labs never totally cracks the code on how to transfer paradigm-shattering technologies into existing HP businesses. And unlike Bill Hewlett, who could just start a calculator division when the existing businesses refused the calculator opportunity, HP Labs cannot start divisions at this point. As a necessary measure, we become better at transferring technology outside the company, launching new businesses or selling it off.

Engaging the Whole Person

The year 1994 concludes with the annual review. Lab and center directors prepare the usual reports for the new CEO, Lew Platt, and his staff on what happened last year and what will happen next year. It's so ordinary! And so not "world's best"!

Sukumar and I ask Joel, "Why not replace the usual slide-slapping mind-numbing presentations about our past and future technologies? Why not present our top three MC^2 visions? John Young (our former CEO) once said, 'HP Labs is like a beach boardwalk for executives—full of great rides and amazing things to take in.' Why not play that one out using HP the Medical Company, HP the Digital Imaging Company, and HP the Telecommunications Company? Involve the whole person, the whole executive, in our thinking. Create theme-park experiences that bring our visions to life. Hook the kid inside each of them and pull that energy and perspective into our strategic discussions."

Joel is skeptical, but keeps listening and agrees to a compromise. We'll do both: in the morning, an abbreviated traditional approach; in the afternoon, the theme-park approach.

Previewing these scenes the night before, Joel asks, "Are you sure this will work? It's not too late to cancel. They aren't expecting anything like this, so they won't miss it." We try to reassure him it's going to be great, and then point out that the whole company has got to take more risks—as he constantly points out. So, some risks will fail. This may be one of them. He can honestly say, he left it up to the best judgment of his managers.

Joel leaves feeling a little better, we hope. Sukumar and I then stay up three more hours obsessing before we surrender to the possibility that this may be a disaster—but at least we will have modeled risk taking! Suk and I think about Gandhi's words "Be the change you want to see." That's part of putting a stake in the ground. This night it feels like putting a stake in our hearts.

Radical Stand

BE THE CHANGE
YOU WANT TO SEE

The next day I shadow Lew Platt, our CEO and Joel's boss, as he walks into "HP the Medical Company," the dramatic rendition of a possible HP future driven by our potential with medical technologies. He looks around at the skeleton hanging in the back of the room, at the two lab directors in white coats and stethoscopes, takes a seat, removes his jacket, loosens his tie, stretches his legs, and in fifteen minutes is involved in a heated debate about HP's future as a medical company. Not traditional annual-review behavior!

Lew later tells Joel that this is the best review he's ever attended, and that HP Labs is giving him the information he and his staff need to really do their jobs, to figure out what kind of company HP should be five years from now. Lew and his staff take slides from the presentations and weigh these visions of the future for the next six months. As I mentioned earlier, then all three visions turn into major MC^2 businesses for HP within the next three years and drive collaborative work across our centers and labs as high as 40 percent. Silos are a thing of the past!

I find myself musing on all this. By engaging the whole person—both in the imaginative creation of the theme-park rooms and the left-brain/right-brain involvement by the CEO and his staff—we seem to have tapped into much greater creativity for strategic decision making. How much we lose when we come only from that passionless subset of ourselves we know as "the professional."

Doubt Scratches at My Door

Being "in charge" of the WBIRL project, I am very excited

by our thirty-six work groups and tell their stories at a dozen coffee talks around HP Labs as my year-end report on WBIRL. Many people are excited about what they hear, but many others listen with blank stares. Probing, I learn they're bored, cynical, and a few think I'm ripping these groups off somehow, claiming their work as my own. I also hear, "We already are the best and just need a marketing department," and "If we were serious about becoming 'world's best,' would we put Personnel in charge of it? We don't need cheerleaders!"

In spite of many wonderful results, I go in and out of deep doubts about what I'm doing. The cynical comments hurt. Senior management push-back hurts. Sometimes I feel like a fraud. I'm often introduced as being "in charge," yet I'm not classically in charge of anything. Others are doing all the work. My role seems to be to create mirrors to show the whole what the parts are doing—through coffee talks and small meetings, and by networking people with similar or complementary ideas. That, and providing small grants out of my budget. So maybe I *am* ripping others off? Should I be doing something that feels more like "work"? I go home at the end of a day, exhausted after ten hours or more, and can't think of one tangible thing I've done.

And can it really be okay that I don't have a high-level plan for making HP Labs the world's best industrial research lab? That I haven't persuaded top management to drive this effort from the top?

Looking back, with the help of a brilliant consultant and friend Kristin Cobble, I see that consulting on behalf of a self-organizing transformation requires a disconcerting break from a more traditional approach.

Traditionally, consultants and leaders know a lot and do a lot. They design and facilitate off-sites, charter business-process re-engineering teams, develop plans that cascade down through the organization, and track systems to make sure all goes as planned. Scorecards report results against the past and sometimes against plans.

In the case of self-organizing transformation, Joel as the "leader" and I as the change manager begin by *not knowing* what WBIRL might be or how HP Labs might get there or even if it should. This creates a huge empty field on which others are invited to play at any level they choose. Joel and his staff create and implement only the plan for which they are personally responsible. By example they invite others to do the same. A third of the labs sign up with no direction other than modeling from above.

No one is driving this effort. It doesn't need anyone to drive it. This is life organizing to get life's work done. All you do is try to encourage life wherever you find it, and organization will follow.

And my job as change manager seems to be doing nothing more, nor less, than listening, mirroring, making the whole visible to the parts, and feeding visibility, money, and time to what wants to happen.

Things that keep me going this first year when I'm doubting everything:

- Joel is bigger than all my doubts about the process and about myself. Constant in his belief that we're making progress, he urges the WBIRL intention in all major projects, offers substantive input to the process, and consistently recognizes me for my efforts. (It's amusing and sometimes frustrating to us both that we never do figure out how to describe my role. He calls me his right hand, his star quarterback, the spirit of change, the heart of HP Labs. None of these fit any known HP job description, so the annual Personnel "cleanup" of weird jobs always catches me in its maw.)

- I experience the passion coming through the people who show up to play and now can see just how we can take this self-transformation all the way to my ultimate goal, stewardship of the planet.

Radical Stand

USE OBSTACLES
AS INFORMATION

- I force myself to ask of every obstacle, "What if this is a gift? What is it that this obstacle or setback is *telling* me?" Ed Karrer, the center director originally most skeptical of the WBIRL effort, becomes my best partner, constantly detecting the hype and fluff and unnecessary complexity in my thinking about what we are doing and what the next steps are.

- I start seeing visionaries everywhere. I ask them how they keep going in the face of the ridiculous disparity between their dreams and reality. I discover deep spirituality all around me among people I've been working with for years.

- A network emerges that cradles me when I'm down. There are five offices within a ten-minute walk where I can cry, curse, collapse, and get buoyed up for the next round. Cheryl Ritchie, who is our communications manager, and Sukumar can be counted on to give me wry acknowledgment and confirm I'm not crazy; Eugenie Prime, HP's library director, starts in with her wonderful Trinidadian accent, *"Bab, never forget how wonderful you are!"*; Laurie Mittelstadt brings tea and sympathy at any moment; and if it's a sleepless night, I can always call Bristol and catch our university-relations manager, Catherine Slater, for reminders of the fat sheep she saw on her last holiday; or count on Ian Osborne, the Bristol operations manager, for one-upmanship in the outrageous-corporate-behavior department.

• Sandra Florstedt, my creative consultant friend, puts me in her car and takes me to see her buddy Roger Harrison, an elder in the consultant community and a pioneer of "whole systems" work. I tell him what I'm doing and how strange it feels. I share my deep misgivings and ask him if he thinks I'm actually doing anything at all.

Radical Stand

KEEP THE FAITH

He says, "You are at the edge of our knowing. It's okay. It's okay to feel like you're about to fall off that edge. Trust your instinct. It's right. What you are doing is pioneering work. Document it. We need to know what you are learning."

Moving into Year Two

The results of the 1994 Employee Survey show significant improvement in all major categories, despite the fact that the previous survey showed the best results we'd ever had!

Now in my second year of having a budget, I formalize this "budget for the people" into the WBIRL Grants Program. And now I ask for matching funds from applicants where possible. Why? First, my budget goes further. Second—and much more important—it requires line management to learn about and co-own the efforts of their people. Finally, my matching funds become a benign incentive for the organization to redirect money from old priorities to new ones.

In addition to ongoing groups, new work groups spring up from all levels. For example, Long Yang, an engineer, asks me after my 1994 year-end report, "Why can't engineers decide what basic research to do? Why do we have to do what senior management says?" I say, "I don't know," and immediately start wondering how on earth I can fix this problem. Then I remember to ask, "Got any ideas how to make it happen?"

A month later, with matching funds from me and the centers, the Grassroots Research Grants Program begins with $120,000. It is entirely owned and operated by engineers, soliciting proposals from other engineers and funding 6 to 8 "out of the box" research projects a year. The peer-review process, championed by Nick Moll and Alan Karp, two senior technical contributors who volunteer to help as the program matures, gets incorporated into other areas of research, and the program is adopted in the ongoing line budget two years later. It is still going in the new millennium in both HP Labs and its spin-off, Agilent Labs.

By the end of this second year, the WBIRL program has proved itself. It's here to stay for at least the five years we intended, and so am I.

Oddly, at this relative height of success, I feel dispirited, down. Among those who aren't on board, there's a lot of muttering along the lines of "Who cares if we're world's best?" With dread in my heart, I discover I am more in alignment with those who mutter than with those excited about the changes.

Part of the problem is, if you focus on becoming the best in the world, you really just end up in an improvement process at best—and behind, in any case. You look at what you are doing, you look at what the other companies are doing, and you come up with a tactical plan to get from here (excellence) to there (the world's best as they were when you benchmarked them, but by the time you implement, they will have moved on). It is not breakthrough. It is not reinventing the game.

I confess my dirty little secret to Joyce Dowdall, a consultant from the Generative Leadership Group who I've hired to coach me during this transformation: "This vision is just not lighting the place up anymore—and it's not lighting me up, either."

She says, "Becoming WBIRL isn't big enough. You need a vision so big it will require all the individual visions to accomplish it. You'll never evoke people's best efforts with your current vision, and you aren't even going to evoke your own best work."

With a sinking feeling, I know she's right. Our vision needs serious help.

Losing My Hearing, Finding My Listening

My doubts about our vision are literally ringing in my ears. It's March 1995 and I have had ten attacks of prostrating vertigo, vomiting, and exhaustion in the last year and a half. After exams for sinus infections, inner-ear infections, and brain tumors, they diagnose Ménière's disease. It seems I will go deaf; they suggest I learn to lip-read while I can still hear. As I can't remember anything the expert says after this, I look up Ménière's on the Web and am terrified. To my utter shock, it seems I may join the community of the deaf and hard of hearing.

With remorse, I suddenly see that I have viewed deaf and hearing-impaired people through the eyes of pity and have seen them as infinitely distant from myself. I e-mail friends in the group and am told to visit the Ear Institute. Tests confirm what I already know: that I am indeed losing my hearing. I can no longer hear whole sections of the sound spectrum. The part of the spectrum where most men's voices fall is almost completely out of my range.

On some level, even in my horror, I think it's funny that this radical feminist can no longer hear most men's voices, unless I sit very close to them and listen with great intensity—in other words, unless I really, really want to hear them and they let me sit close!

I take this illness to mean that I have listened too much to men's voices and not enough to my own. Now the only voice I can hear in this new and thundering silence, apart from the intermittent ringing, is my own. I think about the fact that almost all my meetings consist of almost all men.

But instead of listening to my own voice now, I run from specialist to specialist—ironically all men—unable to decide what to do. Finally, I take a medical leave for a month, just to listen to myself, to tune in so I can understand what I am to do. I see a therapist and cry through every $120 session.

What comes up is deep despair about the gap between what I and even my co-conspirators are able to do, and what needs to be done. On the scale of the world. On the scale of the company. On the scale of family.

On the scale of the family is overwhelming grief at the light going out in my children's eyes, overwhelming grief at my apparent powerlessness to stop it.

In therapy I recall a recurrent dream I have of packing up the family and moving to the West Indies. I've never met a West Indian who didn't think they could change the world if they wanted. Eugenie Prime, the director of the HP research library, is my "prime" example. She and her thirteen siblings come from a Third World community in Trinidad and Tobago, and they are all outstanding: They are doctors, nurses, professors, even "the nose" (one of her brothers is a world-class *parfumier*).

These are black people who stand tall, laugh loudly, and look at each other and white people without defensiveness or suspicion, but without naïveté either. Their ancestors have not known three hundred years of American slavery. They knew British slavery, but it was shorter, provided for an exceptional school system and infrastructure, and then ended. American oppression continues to oppress.

I join a Ménière's support group, fire all the specialists who won't talk to each other (or me), and cobble together my own protocol from stories on the Web. My self-prescribed treatment includes acupuncture, psychotherapy, allergy shots, avoiding dairy and wheat, and regular exercise. It works! I find my balance again and experience no more attacks.

I also buy tickets for a family vacation to Eleuthera, an

island in the Bahamas that is 95 percent black—more so than any island I've researched in the West Indies.

We have a blast. In this place, my son is seen—for the first time—as a handsome, bright, and funny boy. And even more wonderful, as normal.

A Chance to Speak My Truth

I am asked to keynote the '95 Technical Women's Conference. I agree to this during one of my Ménière's attacks, knowing it will force a kind of reckoning for me with HP. I cling to my vision of the corporate sector stepping up to stewardship for the planet and HP leading the charge. At the same time, the reality in the corporate sector and even in HP is so far from the vision. Holding onto it comes at a terrible price to my body, but it feels to me that letting go would cost even more.

For several months, writing my speech feels like making a choice between a rock and a hard place. On the rock side, I can deliver a talk that is really honest, and sobering, but also very depressing. Because it seems to me that our companies are like two hundred-pound teenage boys: their size and strength have far surpassed their intelligence and conscience. They break and hurt things on our precious planet with every move, and they keep eating and fouling things, and they're growing even that much faster, proportionate to their intelligence and conscience. It feels like if I give this talk, it will be my swan song. Surely I wouldn't be able to or even want to stay on afterward.

Choosing the hard place, on the other hand, I can be upbeat, do a great, rollicking, happy talk, but fundamentally lie. I will leave HP if this is the best I can do. I decide to speak my truth.

Writing has always helped me through the hard places, so I start writing. I write an early draft of this book. It takes the form of a paper based on my experience of the corporate sector and my company in particular. I review the "balance sheet."

On the minus side, is there a woman or minority in HP who seriously aspires to become the CEO of this company? I doubt it. Based on my own experience and that of hundreds of other women and minorities I've talked with, any woman or person of color who thinks she's going to become our CEO in a few years would have to be crazy. This is a crying shame. And it's still the case more often than not that unless a sympathetic white male colleague repeats our insights in a meeting, we are not heard. These experiences over time sap our skills, erode our souls, and break our bodies. I am sick of it. Very, very sick in fact.

On the plus side, we have a Technical Women's Conference. And space and time—for which we have fought and won—to gather, thousands strong, to tell the truth as we see it, and dream our dreams for HP's future, and network with each other and with the men we work with to realize those dreams. And this is amazing. *Catalyst* thinks so. The *Wall Street Journal* thinks so. Even *Cosmopolitan* thinks so.

Also on the plus side, if I am honest, it is an amazing fact that I am never penalized for telling the truth in this company, not even when I contradict my manager and won't back down, or even when I contradict the CEO. In fact, I am rewarded for it, time and again, with money, opportunities, and the best friends I have.

As I write my reckoning, I also read a new book that's just come out, Dave Packard's *The HP Way: How Bill Hewlett and I Built Our Company*. I learn that I am part of a tradition that goes way back. Dave tells of personally canceling Chuck House's project on a display monitor for oscilloscopes. In total disagreement, Chuck continues the project as a skunk-works (a hidden project), then persuades some of his friends in manufacturing to make it. He sells seventeen thousand monitors and makes $35 million for the company. When Dave finds out, he bestows upon Chuck a medal for "extraordinary contempt and defiance beyond the normal call of engineering duty."

Asked about rewarding insubordination, Dave says the difference between insubordination and entrepreneurship is intent. As Chuck puts it, "I wasn't trying to be defiant. I just wanted a success for HP. It never occurred to me I might lose my job."

So I add it all up and I find I passionately want HP to survive. When it's all said and done, HP remains the best place I've ever worked, including organizations that I helped create, a few of which turned out to be pretty awful at times.

Radical Stand

REMEMBER WHO
YOU WORK FOR

So I start writing the truth, exactly as I've written about it in my journal, the pluses and the minuses. And a strange thing happens. I also write about beating the diversity goals at the division and corporate levels. I write about the budget-reform initiative. I write about my children and my children and my partner and co-parent, Stacy Cusulos. And I find in the writing that I really want to be right where I am: inside one of the best companies there is, inside a company that *could* step up to lead the whole corporate sector to a new and higher stewardship for the planet. I want us to make it happen. I believe now more than ever that we can do it.

I close my keynote talk with something that's come up for me many times with women and men who come to see me about their careers, and what they can do to advance themselves or HP. I challenge them and myself:

"I have come to believe that to ask, 'What can we do for HP?'—while a necessary question—is not *the* question. Why? Because it confines us to HP as it is, and to existing jobs as the channel for our dreams. This is unworthy of us. We are bigger than this. Much bigger and much more powerful."

I urge us all to go to a larger context. "I believe the critical question before us today is not, What can we do for HP? but rather, What can HP do for the world through us?

"The dream of our founders was to make a contribution to the world. In fact, the contribution that Bill Hewlett was most proud of was no technology or product we ever sold, but the HP Way—the radical belief that people fundamentally want to do the right thing and need only the tools and the support to do it.

"Now it is our turn to ask, what contribution can *we* make to our beautiful, suffering, fragile world and its precious people?

Radical Tool

GO TO A LARGER
CONTEXT

Radical Stand

PUT A STAKE IN
THE GROUND

What are we uniquely positioned to do? What can our life-giving, life-enabling technologies contribute? What destructive ends can we divert them from? What might we do through our citizenship objective if we identified beyond the relatively well-off people of the HP plant to the global village that is now home?

"I propose that these be the contributions we dream of. For *we* are now the founders—of the future HP."

I get hundreds of responses to this talk, beginning with the minute I stop talking. The first person up to me is a male general manager who has tears in his eyes. He hugs me and says, "This is the best damn talk I ever heard and everybody in this company has gotta hear it." A number of women say they had decided to leave HP and will now stay. Two thank me for using the *P* word, "partner," from an HP podium for the first time. Two say they disagree there will never

Radical Move

RECRUIT CO-CONSPIRATORS

be a woman CEO in our time. And they personally aspire to the job!

Five years later, they will prove my pessimism wrong when Carly Fiorina accepts HP's offer, leaves Lucent Technologies, and becomes the only female CEO in the Fortune 200. Thirteen months into her leadership, revenues are up 15 percent and earnings have jumped a startling 23 percent.

Chapter 5

BEING BEST FOR THE WORLD

How I'd thought it worked was, if you were great, like Martin Luther King Jr., you had a dream. Since I wasn't great, I figured I had no dream and the best I could do was follow someone else's. Now I believe it works like this: It's having the dream that makes you great. It's the dream that produces the greatness. It's the dream that draws others around us and attracts the resources it takes to accomplish the dream.

i keep thinking about what Joyce Dowdall has said to me, that our vision of becoming the World's Best Industrial Research Lab isn't big enough. That we need a vision so big that fulfilling it requires the fulfillment of the individual visions of every one of HP Labs' now eleven hundred employees.

At the same time, I am also trying to organize our division's annual review—of course, I want to do it not just as the usual top-down, slide-slapping presentation, but to make it a participatory event, a town meeting, co-created by the employees. We've downsized so much, consolidated so much, everybody is doing so much more than they used to and working much longer hours. Not many make the time to help out, but a planning committee of folks who care does come together, from HP Labs groups worldwide.

I put Joyce's comment on needing a bigger vision to the committee and ask them to think about what that vision might be. Later, Laurie Mittelstadt drops by my cubicle and muses,

"Being the best industrial research lab *in* the world doesn't do it for me. But I'd get up in the morning to be best *for* the world." We both immediately light up. It's just a 2 percent tweak to our old vision, but it makes all the difference in the world.

Radical Tool

TWEAK,
DON'T TOSS

I run around over the next few weeks hawking this vision and getting feedback.

It's a hit! The vision is contagious, the excitement electric, and the committee works far beyond our original intentions and commitments. The event has grown into an annual review *plus* town meeting, which we are calling "A Celebration of Creativity," and where we'll propose our vision to all of HP Labs.

A senior scientist, Sid Liebes, plays around on his computer one night when he can't sleep, trying to design a poster for the celebration. He does some sketches and writes up his plan for a poster that includes twenty to thirty small pictures illustrating the evolution of life on this planet. It ends with a scene that shows Bill and Dave looking into the tiny garage where they started their company—but now the garage is filled by an image of our beautiful blue Earth, the shot taken from the Apollo spacecraft. Emblazoned across the top of the garage are the words "HP for the World." An administrative assistant on our committee, Rhonda Kirk, who moonlights as an artist, looks over Sid's ideas and convinces us to just use one of those images—the last one—as our poster. We do, and we get Bill and Dave to autograph it.

The image of "HP for the World" is the logo for the annual review, but it soon takes on a life of its own. (It's what business guru Seth Godin calls an "ideavirus," an idea so compelling and fun that it spreads like lightning.) We are getting requests from all over the company for the poster, and our two thousand extra copies are soon gone. So we put the image on the HP Web site as a JPEG file. And we give it to the HP company store, which immediately puts it on mouse pads, T-shirts, and coffee mugs.

We tailor the Celebration of Creativity around this vision and, finally, the event for which we've so long planned takes place in October 1995. Eight hundred Palo Alto employees pour into a tent we've had to build in the parking lot—we've never been under one roof before because there is no place at HP big enough. We are live-linked to our three hundred colleagues in Bristol, who are just ending their day. Delegates from the Japan labs have flown in.

We kick off with a Readers' Theater sharing the exciting evolution from "best *in* the world" to "best *for* the world." Dave Packard talks to us about the power of teamwork to produce the impossible. Our CEO, Lew Platt, points to the celebration itself as the proof and power of HP Labs' teamwork. And Joel calls it yet one more manifestation of what the Best Industrial Research Lab for the World can do when challenged. Bill Hewlett adds his kudos from the audience. This is one of the last times Bill and Dave will be together, ever.

A town meeting follows, where we ask everyone to scale down the concept of "HP for the World"

Radical Tool

HOLD UP
A MIRROR
VIA READERS'
THEATER

Radical Tool

SCALE DOWN,
THEN SCALE
BACK UP

and consider, What does "HP for the World" mean for *me*? What does it mean in my life? In my work? How do I want to contribute to this vision? Then we ask them to scale the vision back up, step by step, by asking themselves, What does "HP for the World" mean for my group? For HP Labs? For HP as a company? And what does it mean for the world?

People who never even venture a question in a coffee talk are suddenly pouring out their hearts with their dreams of a better world and their ideas about how to make it happen. David Sibbet, our keynote listener from Joel's management off-site, is back, listening the entire division and many of our friends into an eight-by-forty-foot mural of our collective dream of "HP for the World." Out of this town meeting comes renewed energy for all our work, and new projects aimed at contributions in medicine, education, and the environment.

We notice that energy and creativity surge when the context for people's work scales up. The excitement spreads across the company. In the next year, our "HP for the World" logo is purchased by fifty thousand employees—on T-shirts, mugs, mouse pads, and posters. It is used in ads for HP, it appears in the Canadian *Globe and Mail*; it shows up on the CEO's gifts to his colleagues at other companies, at all of HP's recruiting events, at the HP booth at the National Urban League Conference, and on the HP credit union's Visa card! HP Sweden does a little digital magic, substituting fir trees for California rosebushes beside the garage, dusts the whole scene with snow, adds icicles, and sends it out as its holiday greeting card.

"HP for the World" becomes the banner uniting all our businesses, rooting our present and future in the legacy of

Bill and Dave. The year concludes with a sense of large-scale transformation. A former director of HP Labs calls out from his stand in the bleachers under the Palo Alto tent, "HP Labs has never been so good!"

The third year of HP Labs' self-transformation continues the momentum of vision with twenty new projects and the follow-on to the Celebration of Creativity. As a result of the town meeting, discussion begins on a sensor net for worldwide environmental monitoring, work accelerates on remote medical care for the Third and First Worlds, and new investigations begin on breakthrough technologies for education. The work on the sensor net will never become a business despite its complete feasibility: There is no division to which to transfer it. Remote medical care for emerging countries fails to materialize; its champion takes his ideas off to another company. The new investigations on breakthrough technologies for education will eventually scale up into a full business.

Deciding to ask for the impossible, I point out to the senior managers during an early-morning staff meeting that the last bastion of our hierarchical and information-hoarding past is the exclusive strategic off-sites we hold. Until we open these up to everyone, we will never unleash the creativity of our people. I fully expect this agenda item to take one minute or less, since it's preposterous to think that the senior staff will agree to open up its off-site to the entire division.

To my astonishment, they discuss the idea seriously and resolve that if the security issues can be worked out, the entire off-site should be held on the Web, real time, for anyone in our technology labs who wants to participate. Sometimes, people refuse to live down to our lowest expectations!

Bina Shah, our communications manager in Bristol, and her work-study student Mathias Willerup step up to the security challenge, and work round the clock for weeks to pull it off. It's a resounding success—thirteen thousand hits on the first day alone as employees tune in, give their input, and follow up on discussions.

The voice of HP Labs employees scales up again with the founding of the Community Forum, a self-organizing group of engineers and those who support them. They create a seminar series, a monthly newsletter that contains interviews with technical people and overviews of new projects, a Web-based HP Labs–wide community calendar, and an exchange program between geographically diverse technology labs.

Radical Tool

SCALE UP

Bringing an Issue Home

I'm driving home listening to my voice mail on the car phone, exhausted and exhilarated after the town meeting on "HP for the World." I almost go off the freeway. My friend Kim Harris in the Gay and Lesbian Employee Network is telling me that the HP executive team has just decided not to offer domestic-partner benefits to the families of gay employees.

I can't believe it. This is in complete contradiction to the company I believe I'm working for. Now "HP for the World" feels like a pipe dream—or worse, a lie. What does "HP for the World" mean if it doesn't start at home?

I hit "reply" and flame on about how unacceptable this

is, then ask Kim to let me know if there's anything I can do to help. He's in my office the next day.

Folks in the network are very discouraged. Some are saying, "We speak up on the issue for over a decade and are given a consolation prize: an invitation to speak to the twenty senior personnel managers six weeks from now and to the CEO and his staff two weeks after that. But we've already said everything there is to say, so why bother, if this is the best they can do?"

Something tells me the problem is that the issue is seen just as *an issue*, not as something that deeply affects flesh-and-blood employees—employees who are doing good work for HP and suffering because of the company's decision. We need to scale down the issue to life at the level of flesh-and-blood employees. I show Kim a tape of the Readers' Theater we'd done the day before to kick off the town meeting for the Celebration of Creativity. We decide to create a new Readers' Theater.

We send out a questionnaire to gay employees and straight friends, beginning with the questions How has homophobia affected your productivity? and What business issue would you rather be discussing with the CEO and his staff than homophobia? I ask everyone to tell the truth. If it seems too dangerous to go public

Radical Stand

PUT A STAKE IN
THE GROUND

Radical Move

TAP THE
STRENGTH
OF YOUR
RELATIONSHIPS

Radical Tool

SCALE DOWN

Radical Tool

HOLD UP
A MIRROR
VIA READERS'
THEATER

with it, we can edit, change names, etc., for the final script. People can read each other's stories.

Stories from gays and straight friends come in from around the world. One woman living in a very conservative town asks to remain anonymous—fifteen miles away a lesbian couple has been burned to death in their home. The rest ask to have their names and work sites mentioned. I arrange the stories thematically into a Readers' Theater piece and add a Greek chorus in the background that reads out the litany of names of HP's competitors who are already offering domestic partner benefits.

The nerve-wracking day arrives. The thirteen of us reading stories include a marketing manager, a site-services manager, a general manager who has "come out" because he believes he has to; and several new college recruits from our best schools.

We perform our play for the personnel managers, and for a moment believe our worst fears have been realized when nobody says a word after we finish. The silence seems to go on forever. Finally, Susan Bowick, soon to become HP's new VP of Personnel, says tearfully, "I'm so moved, I can't say anything." Pete Peterson, current VP of Personnel says, "This is great. Exactly what we've needed." Then comes the applause, and questions and comments pour out.

Radical Tool

TURN "ENEMIES"
INTO ALLIES

Seeing the high-level issue of homophobia scaled down to individual stories of how people's lives are interrupted and made less productive by it brings the issue home. Even a manager adamantly opposed to "the lifestyle" tells us, "Oh,

I don't want this to be happening to you. This isn't the HP Way."

We get strong support from many of these senior personnel managers. We get ongoing coaching and support from our diversity manager, Emily Duncan, who works day and night behind the scenes dealing with employees and managers who do not believe the company should reverse its decision and who confuse providing equal pay (and benefits) for equal work with approving the lifestyle.

Radical Tool

SCALE DOWN

We go on to share our stories with the CEO and his staff in the boardroom—and what was billed as a half-hour agenda item turns into one and a half hours. The play allows Lew Platt and his staff to scale down from the abstractions of "employee benefits," "diversity," and "homophobia" to the day-to-day obstacles that "real employees" face just to do our jobs. According to several in the audience who talk to me later, the most stunning thing about the performance is the way we look: "like real employees."

Lew amplifies our message by encouraging us to perform the play down the chain of command. Almost every senior vice president—they are all men—asks us specifically to perform the play for his own staff.

We do, gladly. In addition, we send the floppy disk of the script to all the chapters of the Gay and Lesbian Employee Network, updating them on our performances, the responses, and our next steps; and inviting them to edit and use the script, removing and adding stories that render it more appropriate to their own setting.

Between the top-down and the bottom-up performances, and with the behind-the-scenes support of our diversity and personnel managers, we perform sixty times in six months, and the company reverses its stand—even though it had said it would not reconsider its decision for at least a year.

As a result, HP is providing its people a community of a much higher quality than the towns—or countries—in which many of us live. In fact, when this policy is rolled out, there are country managers who call and say, "Look, it's against the law in this country to recognize these relationships." And the HP response is, "Well, inside our walls, we recognize these relationships. And in our benefits policies, we are going to recognize these relationships and these families."

My friends in many of the religious denominations are still slogging it out on this issue. Like many other global companies, HP has driven a wedge—and affirmed that the potential for global companies to do good is awesome. Today, HP stock is favored in socially conscious portfolios, and the company can recruit and retain people with the best skills, regardless of a candidate's or employee's family constellation.

Being Blind to Treasure

None of us is exempt from the kind of thinking the HP executive board had been doing before our play: seeing "the other guy" as just that. Other. Different from "us." Not as worthy.

Sadly, I do it all the time.

One day we are planning a Labs team-building event and someone says, "Hey, Barb. Rolf Jaeger is a musician. You should ask him to play."

I groan inwardly. Rolf is a physicist at HP Labs and I have consigned Rolf to my nerd bucket: very bright, distant, sarcastic, cynical, and unavailable for anything I'll ever think of. I know he'll refuse to play. But it's my job to ask, so I do. True to my expectations, he says no. (People do live down to our expectations, I find.)

I find some other background music for the event, including the segment where we invite managers to share their personal photos. (Bill Hewlett offers his photos of wildflowers, a lifelong passion for him.)

After the event, Rolf comes up to me and says, "You asked me to play for the wrong thing."

"What do you mean?"

"You should have asked me to play for the wildflower collection. "

"Oh," I reply. "What kind of music do you do?"

"I'll give you a tape."

I think, okay, well, whatever, and go on about my business.

A few days later, the tape shows up on my desk. I resent that I now have to listen to it. But then I take a look. It looks pretty interesting. There is a lovely watercolor of a lake on the front. I think, *That's odd, I wonder what kind of music this is.* So on the way home, I pick up the tape and reluctantly shove it into the cassette deck. A rich musical texture fills the car.

I almost drive off the road. This music is so mind-bendingly beautiful, I am blown away. One of the songs, "Baby Eric," which Rolf wrote for his son, has me in tears. It is so moving, I pull off the road.

The next day I call Rolf and tell him I am awestruck by

his tape. Can I get more? Can I use them? He is excited by my excitement, and the next thing I know I've got a pile of tapes ("Eternal Voyage," "Sonic Metamorphosis," "Mind & Soul"), all featuring the same style of watercolor on the front.

It turns out that Rolf's music has been used at spiritual events and global healing celebrations for years. The radiant landscapes on the front are by his father, Klaus Jaeger, who is a German Expressionist painter.

I end up using Rolf's music at HP Labs workshops, for my personal meditation, even as the background music for a major conference. For one event, Rolf writes a special piece.

From then on, anything Rolf is involved in, I want to be involved in: He is landscaping a garden for a homeless shelter, and I go along with other HP volunteers to help. I discover in Rolf—when I get past the stereotype that's killed him for me—an incredibly warm, generous, and loving spirit.

Radical Tool

PLAY WITH
WHOEVER
SHOWS UP

The point is, we don't know who we're at work with. We underestimate each other, especially when we see them as "them." We don't begin to understand the magnificence that could be available if we can see each other outside the boxes of our org charts and cubicles. Had I not asked Rolf to help out, risking rejection, had he not reached back, risking rejection, we would have completely missed each other—and the valuable co-conspirator we found in each other.

From Stardust to Us

A few weeks after the "HP for the World" town meeting,

senior scientist Sid Liebes, who created the globe-in-the-garage graphic, drops by my cube. "My dream 'for the world' has been to create a one-mile walk through time. The last five billion years scales beautifully to a mile—it's a million years a foot!" He is so excited. "I had this dream twenty-seven years ago when I was a professor—it came to me on the first Earth Day. I just got in touch with it at the town meeting and now I'm determined to do it."

Sid's manager, Bill Shreve, a great WBIRL supporter, had recently asked him what he wanted to do in the years left before his retirement. Sid had told him about his dream of the walk through time and Bill replied, "If you can get WBIRL to pay for it, I'll keep paying your salary and take care of your team."

Radical Tool

I am thrilled. Of course we'll figure out how to pay the costs. This is great!

SCALE DOWN

Sid is incredulous. "Why would HP want to build a wall with the story of life on it?" I counter, "Well, no one is going to give you the money to go build a brick wall till you can show them a prototype. Let's do a paper wall first. Besides, the HP Labs thirtieth birthday is coming up. We'll use that as an excuse to create the timeline."

Despite misgivings, Sid agrees to stay and manage the project. We create a fabulous scaled-down version of Sid's Walk Through Time—still a mile long, but a gallery of posters.

Using HP DesignJet printers to print beautiful three-by-five-foot poster-size graphics, a team that grows to more than one hundred HP employees and thirty outside consultants, artists, scientists, and museum exhibitors creates an exhibit of eighty-eight panels that illustrate the evolution of life from stardust to us and put people in touch with the miracle of life, the mass extinction that our human species has precipitated, and the awesome responsibility and possibility of the moment. We will learn later that up to that point, no one has told the story integrating all the latest findings made possible by new technologies.

As the team gets bigger and the Walk Through Time gets more exciting, senior management, who originally agreed to the idea, begins to question why HP Labs is spending its research dollars/pounds/yen on an environmental statement. Then the PR folks at Corporate get word of the project and say, "Hey! What are you doing? HP hasn't even taken a public position on the environment yet."

I am discouraged. I talked Sid into staying with HP to do this project, and now what? The night after the fourth such call from on high, I go to bed and tell the Great Spirit, "You gotta handle this one, because I don't know what to do. I can't imagine we've come this far in creating this story, just to shut it down."

Radical Stand

REMEMBER WHO
YOU WORK FOR

The next day I wake up at 4:00 A.M. with the realization of how we can pull this thing off. Instead of presenting the Walk Through Time as content—that is, an environmental statement, we can reframe it as the context in which we should ask our greatest business questions.

I go back to everyone and say, this isn't a content statement—we're not saying we're the company that's leading on the environment, we're not saying what we should or shouldn't do. We're saying, here's a scientific version of the way life came to be and here's the way it looks right now, and our company is a major player with regard to the future of life.

Radical Tool

REFRAME THE CONTEXT, GO TO A LARGER CONTEXT

The Walk Through Time is about giving people the chance to experience Earth's history, thus creating the most powerful context we can for asking business questions. How do we want to play as a company with respect to the future of life? What should we be working on? How should we work? Why should we be in the markets we're in? What else might we be doing?

Once we reframe the project this way, opposition to the Walk almost disappears—and is replaced by support, imagination, and enthusiasm for the effort. In fact, the Walk Through Time succeeds beyond our wildest dreams.

Completed, it is a magnificent statement about the fragility of life and the precarious moment of "now," and about the profound implications of the decisions we make, consciously or not.

The Walk Through Time becomes the centerpiece for our second Celebration of Creativity, which we hold on Earth Day. HP Labs employees take the walk in Palo Alto, Bristol, and Japan—we've mounted a full set of posters at each location. Bill Hewlett comes by the Palo Alto site and takes the Walk in his wheelchair. So does our CEO, Lew Platt. All come up with great ideas and reflections on the future and the contributions HP can make. The next day, other HP employees take the Walk and add their thoughts to the mix. Everyone's comments are digitally stitched into a "quilt" and put on the HP Web site. Other HP divisions borrow the exhibit and string it across town. Our site in Corvallis, Oregon, puts up the Walk at a local celebration and the whole town has a chance to see it.

The day after the Walk Through Time premieres in Palo Alto, we scale up. Visitors from academia, museums, and other companies—fifty nonprofits in all—are invited to take the Walk. Things really heat up after that, and the State of the World Forum requests we mount the Walk in San Francisco to kick off the deliberations of eight hundred world leaders in a few months. They also invite our CEO to give the keynote. We agree and I share the good news with my friends Juanita Brown and David Isaacs. They suggest we pull together the State of the World Forum staff, Lew Platt's speechwriter, and the Walk Through Time team at their home for a day to imagine the possibilities of this conjunction of forces.

Radical Tool

SCALE UP

Radical Tool

SCALE WAY, WAY UP!

We ask the Forum folks, Jim Garrison and Diane Mailey, "What is the speech you need and haven't heard from a CEO?" They respond, Glenda Dasmalchi takes notes, writes the speech, and Lew—who is renowned for editing and rewriting his speeches, delivers it intact—without reading, as his own. He begins with a point first articulated by CEO Robert Shapiro of Monsanto: "The world will reward the companies that help solve the world's problems." Lew then points out that "doing good and doing well are not mutually exclusive." In fact, he adds, "Doing good may be the best way to do well." Afterward, all eight hundred leaders take the mile-long Walk before they sit down for their discussions on the future of the planet.

The Foundation for Global Community is hugely excited about the possibilities of using the Walk as an educational tool, and we eventually transfer ownership of the exhibit to them. Sid Liebes takes his retirement and works with the foundation to continue to champion the Walk around the world. Requests are coming in fast and furious. The Tech Museum in San Jose mounts the Walk along the river that runs through the city, where one hundred thousand visitors can see it. NASA strings the Walk a mile along Moffett Field in nearby Mountain View.

His first year in so-called retirement, Sid's "dream" and the yearlong effort of a team of more than one hundred is incorporated in its entirety into a handsome coffee table book entitled *A Walk Through Time: From Stardust to Us* and is published by John Wiley and Sons in late 1998. Unfortunately, the remarkable story of HP's contribution is confined to the preface.

The Walk Through Time ends up going all over the world. It becomes a standing exhibit at the Singapore Science Center, where its oversize panels inspire a children's essay contest. It is shown in South Africa for the Parliament of the World Religions. It is purchased by British Petroleum, which shows it to senior managers as well as to the public. The Walk is translated into Spanish and shown in Costa Rica. It is translated into German and plans are made to mount the exhibit in Switzerland and Germany. Australia asks for the rights to put up the Walk themselves and to take it to New Zealand and Japan.

And all because a man with a dream was listened to.

Multiplying One Person into a Movement

One of the hundreds of folks who works on the Walk Through Time is Jim Sheats, a ponytailed scientist who does his HP Labs job during the day and environmental work on evenings and weekends. At the town meeting it occurs to Jim that he could somehow combine the two, and he begins to explore the concept of "technology for sustainability." He applies for—and gets —a grant from my internal WBIRL grants program to devote half his time to the exploration for one year.

Radical Tool

PLAY WITH
WHOEVER
SHOWS UP

After several discussions with Jim, it becomes clear to both of us that there is actually *a lot* of interest at HP in sustainability of the planet, and that his job from one perspective is to identify the people and organizations who are interested, then amplify them.

Radical Tool

AMPLIFY
POSITIVE
DEVIANCE

We decide the best way to strengthen the activity inside the company is to pull all the people who care about sustainability— who are thinly distributed all over the world as "tokens" and surrounded by folks who don't care, or at least don't care as much— into one place for a couple of days. With great excitement, we announce a conference on "HP for Sustainability." We will use this event to amplify our positive deviance, and by choosing to unite, we will take the crucial step of moving from tokens to a minority. Tokens can't change anything, a minority is the only thing that does.

About eight months into our planning, all travel and conferences are canceled, due to companywide expense controls. Our sponsor at Corporate, the head of Product Stewardship, calls me and says, "Barb, we've got to call off the conference. I sure can't cosponsor it—I don't even think I can come. I think you are going to be really at risk if you continue trying to do it."

I agree with everything he's saying, on the one hand, but on the other I think it may just be possible from an HP Labs base. "I really respect where you are coming from and I would be doing the same thing if I worked in your organization. But I feel like we've got to do this now or never. Jim's the passion

Radical Stand

PUT A STAKE IN
THE GROUND

behind it and his one-year grant is expiring, and we've already got all these outside people lined up to come in."

What to do? I know that this time we will lose if we fight this at the level of "Can't our conference be an exception to the rule?" Then I find out that the only thing HP is not canceling is customer visits. Well, some of our keynote speakers are from companies that are key customers, like the executive vice president for business development at 3M. We reframe his coming as a "customer visit," and stretch that term mightily so we can do what we truly believe is in the best interest of the company.

We pull back all of our publicity about the HP for Sustainability conference. We reframe the conference as an

HP Labs customer visit: Customers who work in the sustain-ability domain are coming to talk about what they are doing, perhaps to partner with us into the future. (This is all the right language for customer visits.) Through voice mail and e-mail, we inform the sustainability mavens whom Jim has unearthed from across the company that the event is a cus-tomer visit that's open to anyone in the company who thinks they could benefit from this conversation. We tell them, "In-vite your friends."

The premise of the conference is now successfully re-framed as a way to find real business value with key customers in the issues around sus-tainable development, that is, development that meets the needs of our generation with-out compromising the ability of future gen-erations to meet their own needs.

Radical Tool

REFRAME THE
CONTEXT

Almost none of the HP senior manage-ment we've invited knows anything about the issue (including one who candidly confesses that he came because someone he cared about asked him to make it a pri-ority, and that he thought the conference was on sustaining profit). And absolutely none can make attending the entire two days a priority.

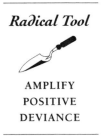

Radical Tool

AMPLIFY
POSITIVE
DEVIANCE

So we ask key folks to attend just one talk (no preparation required) and respond as part of a management panel with their questions and/or thoughts about relevance to HP. This strategy creates the pull for a "briefing on technology and business for sustainability" by sustainability champions in their own organizations, and results in instant engagement, great connections, good quotes for the company newsletter, whose representative attends (thus amplifying our sustainability deviants)—and the kickoff to a whole future for HP and sustainability.

In September 1998, one hundred and fifty people meet for two days to discuss and imagine the future—it is probably the biggest customer visit HP's ever had. Besides presentations by HP customers, we include Native American drumming (courtesy of Marvin Keshner, an HP Labs director in a white shirt and tie, who in his free time is studying drumming with a shaman); my dear friend indigenous healer Lahe'ena'e Gay, who founded the Pacific Cultural Conservancy International, which helps indigenous people preserve their communities and their cultures (she speaks passionately to us about living inside a sustainable culture and what global companies are doing to destroy them); and Stuart Hart, a pioneering business school professor who is working to marry business and sustainability, who discusses the profitability of green thinking.

The "tokens" who come find community and renewed commitment. When someone wonders if the conference is just preaching to the choir, one woman jumps up to insist, "No, there *is* no choir. There are soloists who no longer sing. But we are constituting ourselves as a choir now and I am finding my voice again."

Radical Move

BUILD YOUR CADRE

And it is a very powerful voice. When the HP sustainability deviants disaggregate and go back to their divisions, they're now members of a much larger group—a group that now has its own newsletter, its own Web page, its own conference. Many will soon be featured in a story in the company magazine. A group that has the capacity to call the CEO in and ask him to account for the company in the arena of sustainability.

Our corporate product stewardship and corporate branding functions believe the conference took them places they could not have otherwise gone, and several senior managers commit to exploring appropriate technologies and business models for emerging economies. They follow up with communication sessions to their staffs and field visits to explore options. Chief among those who get it is Lyle Hurst, soon to become a vice president of one of our biggest printing businesses and our biggest champion. Together, these managers demonstrate the message—that one can care about the fragility of the planet *and* benefit the business.

Keeping Fast Company

In early summer of 1998, I get a call from Katharine Mieszkowski. She is doing an article for *Fast Company* magazine. The incredible John Seely Brown at Xerox PARC, whom I met a few months back at a lunch on creativity hosted by Stanford's Michael Ray, has told Bill Taylor, co-founder of *Fast Company,* that they should talk to me. Katharine arrives in jeans and combat boots and we talk for hours. I tell her my story of being a radical and ending up at HP. I tell her about WBIRL and positive deviants and making 2 percent tweaks instead of trying to take great leaps forward, which usually leave a lot of people behind. I stress the importance of starting slow and working small.

Katharine takes voluminous notes and leaves. I don't hear from her for weeks, but I'm not surprised. Clearly we had a good talk and that was that. It's happened before. Somebody tells these writers to talk to me, we have a great talk, and then nothing happens. As a few have called to say later, our great talk didn't exactly fit into what they were doing the article about (change, leadership, women in senior management) or how they think about these topics.

While I'm not surprised nothing is happening, I am disappointed. *Fast Company* was my hope for beginning to spread the word about corporate revolution. *Fast Company* is what you'd get if *Fortune* and *New Age Journal* had a love child. Sort of a new age business journal.

But then the photographer calls to make an appointment, and the fact checker calls to double-check the facts.

The article comes out in December 1998, and I turn out to be the only one in it. Six pages of me. Seems like a lot, but it's great because Katharine leaves nothing out. It will turn out to be the first step in a big scaling up of sharing my own story and the tools I've been using for years.

At the end of the article is my e-mail address. I get a huge response from readers. People want to know how we did this and that and the other thing. I also hear from organizations. *Fast Company* invites me to present at their next conference. Then the Kellogg Foundation contacts me to speak to their eight hundred fellows, who are activists from around the world. The Linkage Leadership Conference, the Linkage Women's Conference, and the Business and Professional Women's Con-

Radical Tool

SCALE UP

THE SOUL IN THE COMPUTER

ference in California ask me to consult on conference planning and to speak.

All that scaling up from one article! And each of these events becomes an opportunity for me to be listened into even more speech. As the audiences to whom I am speaking scale up in size and clout, so does the speaking that they are listening me into.

I always tell basically the same story of change at HP, but when I tell it to eight hundred leaders from around the world, I tell it differently than when I'm telling it to an HP internal audience. With every different audience, I get to develop aspects of what I mean when I say that I am committed to getting the corporate sector to step up to stewardship of the planet.

Not only does the *Fast Company* article give me access to an ever-widening community of corporate revolutionaries, I really don't think I could have ever understood that I *had* a story to tell if not for the listening that came from those groups and new colleagues like Alan Webber, Bill Taylor, Mark Albion, Harriet Rubin, Chris Turner, Bill Strickland, Warren Bennis, and Mike Abrashoff.

Measuring Results

Joel is preparing to retire, but before he leaves, the senior team formally concludes the five-year WBIRL program that has now stretched into six years. What have we actually accomplished?

Both technical and cultural change.

At the highest level, it is now possible to speak of HP Labs as at least *among* the best industrial research labs in and for the world, and some would even say the best. Our vision has scaled up from our division to the company, which now aspires to be the best in and for the world, or, as our wonderful new CEO, Carly Fiorina, will later put it, "the winning e-company with a shining soul."

At the bottom line, HP Labs has created a research agenda that is the envy of many companies. Our resource-allocation process no longer simply extrapolates from the past as it had in our pre-WBIRL history, but is driven by potential futures for the company, futures that it is now HP Labs' business to prototype. We have formal and informal processes in place that ensure cross-disciplinary discovery and invention.

Research results coming out of our agenda reflect unprecedented teamwork across labs and geographies, and new cross-disciplinary synergies. History will be the ultimate judge as to the impact of this explosion of creativity, but here's the tip of the iceberg:

• Our "Wide Word Program" combines expertise from different Palo Alto labs, including physics, logic design, computer architecture, and software engineering. This 64-bit program produces the successor to the PA-RISC architecture developed in HP Labs in the mid-'80s, is compatible with PA-RISC, yet offers breakthrough levels of performance through instruction-level concurrency. As a demonstration of HP's commitment to open source and open systems, the architecture is jointly developed with Intel, and comes to be known as IA 64. The first commercial version is expected to become the open-source post-

RISC 64-bit architecture for PCs and servers throughout the industry. HP will have the advantage of strict binary compatibility, a head start in implementation, and superior compiler technology.

• Our optical switch program uses ink-jet technology to create a scalable, nonblocking optical switch. Switching is performed by the presence or absence of a thermally generated bubble at the intersection of each input and output fiber. By substituting an optical switch for the much slower and more expensive electronic one now in wide use, we provide a critical component in the optical backbone for global high-speed Internet and telecommunications.

• Again using our vast expertise in ink-jet technology, we design a kind of printer that can print gene arrays on chips, substituting the four bases of DNA for the usual inks. Combined with other work we've done in bioinformatic analysis of the human genome, this new business has revolutionary applications in low-cost disease diagnosis, drug development, and drug therapy.

• Customer needs for a database that can scan medium-size databases of telephony call records extremely rapidly lead to the development of a unique database design producing more than a ten-times performance improvement for databases resident in memory. This technology has widespread application for data-mining applications that require rapid analysis of current data, in electronic medical records or service records, for example. When HP decides to get out of the database business, as the industry moves to third-party sourcing, these prototypes spin out into Times Ten, a new database company with customers throughout the industry, including HP.

What remains to be done? To be the best in and for the world is the kind of goal that James Carse, author of *Finite and Infinite Games*, calls "an infinite game." In such a game, the goal is a moving target, a horizon always ahead. You never really arrive because there's always something more and bigger to be done. The only way to lose is to stop playing, but along the way, the point is to create finite games on the infinite playing field. Finite games have goals, competition, winners, and losers.

The biggest finite game ahead comes out of our experience during the WBIRL years. It's a challenge that faces many large companies. Growth slows when current businesses mature. Accelerated growth must come through new businesses that don't extend current businesses—and may even disrupt them. Recognizing the need for nonmatching and disruptive new businesses, the executive committee approves HP Labs' allocation of 30 percent of our resources to technologies and technology combinations that could be commercialized to this end.

However, as a company, we have yet to crack the code on creating in-house, disruptive businesses. Sitting on the shelf are technologies and prototypes for new businesses involving novel eyeglass displays, biosensors for precision agriculture, rear-projection display monitors, rapid-application software development, and . . . The list goes on and on.

All signs point to the need for separate new business organizations, outside the constraints of the current businesses
within the company, dealing with opportunities that have offered the right of first refusal by the existing businesses. Such
opportunities could go in two distinct directions.

If they need the HP brand, the strategic vision of our
CEO, the distribution channels, the service organization, and
HP's investment capability, *and* they promise companywide
impact, these prototypes could be commercialized in a separate new business organization inside HP that would take on
a few of the technologies, and staff and resource them to win.
We've actually succeeded in creating new businesses this way
in the past with the famous HP calculator and the series 700
workstation family. But these efforts have been one-off and
not easily repeated. In the case of the calculator, making it a
reality required Bill Hewlett to start a new division; none of
the existing divisions wanted it. We lack a system and process for churning out the highest growth possible. We have
yet to develop the organizational models with the right degree and levels of support on the one hand, and the necessary autonomy on the other.

If a new technology-driven opportunity would be more
successful in the fast-moving, venture-capital start-up mode,
then HP Labs can partner with a venture capital firm to vet
and commercialize the project in exchange for a share of the
equity for HP. In fact, we are piloting this model of innovation, and the pilots under way look promising.

So the organizational vision, structure, process, and
models for disruptive new-business development remain to
be developed; the organizational will to create them contin-

ues to gestate. The good news is that there are signs everywhere of conception. And HP Labs is in every case one of the parents.

Cultural Changes

The research side is thriving, and so is the culture at HP Labs. In fact, I share with Joel and his staff my growing realization that one of the most important results of all the projects that flowed from the first WBIRL efforts is the cultural change we've inspired.

Before we began, we had pretty much the top-down military model, the heroic form of leadership where the top decrees action that others execute. Now, instead of being implementers of somebody else's vision, employees have become entrepreneurs for their own. And we have a living-system model, where there is much more inquiry, asking questions of each other, and much more relationship.

We can actually measure this aspect of the transformation by the number of groups that have formed, the number of collaborations. We've gone from almost no collaborative work across our silolike technology laboratories to about 40 percent collaboration.

Communication has emerged from a broadcast-down-through-the-system paradigm to a teeming web of communication, with a lot more lateral discussion—plus the techniques and tools to encourage it.

We've gone from no Quality approach at all in the company's central research lab—in fact, it is almost a principle of being in research that you don't have to do Quality (*that* is for manufacturing)—to having more than one hundred projects that are about process improvement or creating something completely new to meet a need that wasn't being met. And we've gone from no research metrics to easily understood and systematically implemented metrics across all of HP Labs.

We've gone from having no vision on any level that anybody could articulate to having one that is rooted firmly at the level of the individual. From there it scales up to the group level, the organization level, the company level, and the world.

And we've gone from really no sense of standing for the world to our CEO saying in front of eight hundred world leaders—and in front of tens of thousands via our Web site—that the corporate sector has got to set a higher standard of stewardship for the planet, and that this is not inconsistent with making a profit.

In fact, as we had hoped he would, and as he said—and as I am shortly to find out—it may be the best way to make a profit.

One Becomes Two

There are some decisions that may be good for business, but are real tough for the people involved. In 1999, Hewlett-Packard makes a number of them.

Taking a look at how the company has evolved, the board of directors recognizes that the computer and instrument sides of the company are evolving into different businesses with different business models. They decide to spin off the forty-three thousand people on the instrument side into a separate company that will come to be known as Agilent Technologies.

Agilent will operate fully independently. It will have its own building, its own personnel policies, its own information technology, board of directors, etc. It will become completely separate.

Many of HP's existing divisions will be transferred whole to Agilent; others, including HP Labs, will be split down the middle. Engineers who are working on projects involving measurement, medical, and components technologies will go to Agilent Labs; engineers who are working on computing and imaging technologies—many of whom have been sitting side by side with the instrument folks for years—will remain with HP. Many partnerships created by Joel's vision of creating MC^2 products and solutions, which combine our measurement, communication, and computing expertise, must now break up.

The churn turns into froth as HP moves into formation as a holding company that has spun off one company, and is now organizing into four more—will these also spin off? When? And how does a central research group support four distinct businesses that no longer have any reason to cooperate? Will we at HP Labs be split up into four more pieces? When? The questions are big, unanswered, unsettling, and produce buzz or stunned stares around the coffee pots. Our budgeting process now involves going to each of the four businesses in HP separately to persuade them they need to support the whole of us. It's a tough sell.

In the meantime, Lew Platt announces his retirement, the search for a new CEO begins, and Joel announces his own retirement and his replacement as director of HP Labs by the team of Dick Lampman and Ed Karrer.

Culture is the operating system of the organization, and all these changes and questions mean big, big change to HP Labs' culture and community. The personnel job is hard. Long hours. Now it's only late at night, through voice mail and weekend e-mails, that I can manage all the scaling-up projects stemming from the grassroots grant program, and HP for Sustainability. I am now the worldwide change manager for the HP Labs/Agilent Labs split. It is a time of complete chaos and churn. On the obvious level, my role is to see that all the subteams required for the split operate in sync, that major milestones and interdependencies are identified, staffed, and tracked. I pull us together once a week over a great lunch to review progress and identify red flags.

Less obvious, and more difficult, my role is to make sure that each new half is emotionally whole—and that throughout the split, the whole community remains whole. Because without wholeness, people don't produce; people leave, spiritually and emotionally, if not physically. And of course, they also leave physically. Retention is a problem.

Our first benchmarking with other companies who have undergone such splits, including other central research labs that have split, reveals a minefield. We are repeatedly assured that we will soon hate each other, be recruiting each others' best people, stealing documents, and worse. We affirm as a team that we are not going down this rat hole.

Upon his retirement, my beloved Joel has ensured that we have the best people in charge. Dick Lampman and Ed Karrer, men of integrity and good friends, are at first the co-directors, and then each the director of an emergent new organization. They model friendship, partnership, and integrity throughout. Toward the end, they throw a party at Dick's house for their direct reports and reaffirm our community and that an organizational split cannot blow it up.

But what about the rest of the organization? There is a lot of sadness and vacant stares as people get it that their friends will have to have signed nondisclosure agreements if they want to plop down and hash out ideas with them in the future.

I talk to my friend and consultant Rayona Sharpnack of my own palpable sadness and grief. A former junior high school teacher and professional softball player, Rayona speaks simply and coaches well. She encourages me to feel what I'm feeling, and then to imagine the possibilities of this moment.

With the help of Rayona and Laurie Mittelstadt, who vets the crazier possibilities I can foresee (but as always comes up with a few that top even mine), I organize a design team to create a short but powerful transition ceremony to help everyone move into the future. Research has shown that when large organizations go through major changes, the people involved have many feelings and thoughts that there is no place to feel or express in the normal course of business. Left unexpressed, their inner experience is carried forward as a heaviness that slows them down and keeps them from moving into the new with enthusiasm.

I take what feels like a big risk, as it does every time I bring my outside interests in. I ask African activist and healer Sobonfu Some to help me with our ritual. (Ironically, I've met her through lab director Marvin Keshner.)

Under a big tent we've again had to build, people sit rapt. The big day has arrived. Sharon Hanrahan, our events planner, and Joan Gallicano, our team-facilities liaison, have outdone themselves, and the food, setting, decorations, and publicity have created enormous expectancy. Three African drummers beat out rhythms as I open by talking about the shock and sadness we experienced in learning about the up-coming split of our community.

Sobonfu alternates with descriptions of her home in Burkina Faso in West Africa and their rituals. "Ceremonies," she tells the audience, "are to the soul what food is to the physical body. They are participatory activities that involve the whole being: body, spirit, mind, and soul. They help us finish with the past; they help us grow into the future." She then tells of her village's birth and delivery celebrations as I interweave the parallels with our own experience of endings and beginnings.

At the end of the ceremony, we hand each person a beau-tiful bronze medallion engraved with the globe-in-the-garage logo on both sides. On one side, the text below the garage reads "HP Labs for the World"; on the other it reads "Agilent Labs for the World." Then we ask each person, "Turn your medallion so your new company is facing outward, but know that whichever company you now work for, the other is close to your heart."

I say, "We go forward as two sides of the same coin. The two sides are the two new labs. Each is whole. Each contains the other. The coin is the legacy of Bill and Dave, the legacy of contribution, of improving the welfare of humanity."

Even the cynics are crying. The day ends with hours of dancing, led by Sobonfu, Ed, and Dick, our usually more reserved lab directors!

The Culture Team

I feel I am moving on—to *what* remains to be seen, but I begin to plan for it. First I recruit the best change manager I know in the company, Ron Crough, to help me launch the reinvention of HP Labs so it aligns with a new, integrated e-services company that's taking shape within HP. I know that Ron's work will soon take on a life of its own and scale up to a point where I can step away from my own change-management role.

The WBIRL programs transmute into new directions, including into a new Culture Transformation team, headed by Howard Taub, our most seasoned HP Labs center director. This team consists of a diagonal slice of the division, and includes WBIRL colleagues like Hazen Witemeyer, Catherine Slater, Sharon Connor, and Laurie Mittelstadt.

Within weeks the group launches an online survey and discussion group that identifies and picks off the low-hanging fruit—like monthly coffee talks, a resurrected chalk-talk series, bike lockers, on-site grocery delivery, and inspiring and informal meeting spaces. For the fruit higher up, the team charters work groups and begins to tackle ranking, recruiting, retention, and sabbaticals.

The infinite game. The beat goes on.

Carly

It's the summer of 1999. Like most people, I am amazed to hear the announcement of our new CEO. "Carly *who*?" is the refrain of the day. Who is she?

Our underground grassroots network turns up inside

information from Lucent Technologies, Carly's former employer, where she was the very successful president of the company's Global Service Provider Business. Before Lucent, she was with AT&T, where she started twenty years earlier as an account executive.

The information we gather includes reports from people who've worked with Carly before. The bottom line is, "She's the real deal." For me, this is amazing good luck—beyond my wildest dreams only a few years ago.

We also discover that Carly is a Renaissance woman. She is a Stanford grad with a degree in medieval history; she is a former law student (as well as a former secretary in a shipping department at HP!); and she holds an MBA from the University of Maryland as well as a master's in science from MIT.

Carly sees many parallels between the Renaissance and our era, especially the ferment of ideas and the possibility for reinventing the world. She believes that technology has the power to transform lives and that our current renaissance, the "Renaissance of the Information Age," as she calls it, could result in the transfer of power to the masses. She also believes that "to the individuals who bring their own spark, their own energy to the process, technology becomes not about bits and bytes, but about the celebration of people's minds and people's hearts."

What will Carly Fiorina allow for that wasn't possible before at HP?

At the company level, she moves for the reintegration of the four remaining businesses, cultivating and exploiting synergies to go after e-services opportunities that no other company can tackle. In concert with this vision, Carly supports a strong central research lab, and the nightmare of HP Labs possibly splitting yet again (into four pieces this time, one for each business) comes to an end.

At the level of my own dreams, and at the level of the world as I envision it, Carly stands for the garage, a garage "for the world," and for our soul, the "soul in the computer." She reminds us of HP's purpose: "Invent for the common good."

In November 1999, Carly and the executive team distill a set of eleven practices from HP's history to serve as a reminder to us of what we stand for, and to challenge us to carry on the legacy of Bill and Dave in ways appropriate to our own time. I don't think of these rules as prescriptive— telling me how to behave. If I did, they'd just inspire my rebellion! No, I think of them as descriptive; they describe and remind me of how things work when they're really working.

Here are the eleven "Rules of the Garage":

1. Believe you can change the world.
2. Work quickly, keep the tools unlocked, work whenever.
3. Know when to work alone and when to work together.
4. Share—tools, ideas. Trust your colleagues.
5. No politics. No bureaucracy. (These are ridiculous in a garage.)
6. The customer defines a job well done.
7. Radical ideas are not bad ideas.
8. Invent different ways of working.

9. Make a contribution every day. If it doesn't contribute, it doesn't leave the garage.
10. Believe that together we can do anything!
11. Invent.

Next Carly formulates a vision for HP as "the winning
e-company with a shining soul." A company with a "shining
soul," she explains, is one with uncompromising integrity. It
is a place whose core values are respect, teamwork, and contribution, and where everyone is a leader. It is a model of
inclusion in the workplace and the marketplace, and it takes
a global leadership role in business and the environment. In
short, it is a company "for the world."

In the summer of 2000, I am sitting in on a small meeting at HP Labs listening to Carly thank one of our teams for
their exceptional work in proposing solutions for a major
customer.

The team had prototyped a customer-relationship management system using integrated state-of-the-art HP technologies (including some still in development) that would take
multiple customers in a family from their first contact with
our client's business through their use of the product and on
into their follow-up experience. Our client is awestruck by
the possibilities that our technology and imagination allowed
for: We are co-inventing a future with them.

Carly tells the HP Labs team that the most important
thing they have done is to manifest *now* the future HP—an
HP where people believe they can do anything, and let nothing stop them.

Having identified the team as positive deviants, a team

that embodies the desired future state for all of HP—that is, doing whatever it takes to help customers realize their dreams—Carly's next step is to amplify them, or as she puts it, "to shamelessly exploit them." She sends folks from all over the company to visit HP Labs and hear the story, see the future they envisioned—not to copy this particular prototype or exhibit, but to discover the team's positive deviant behaviors and practices so

Radical Tool

AMPLIFY POSITIVE DEVIANCE

they can give the same kind of visibility, velocity, and scale to their own passions for customer solutions.

Carly frequently refers to the team in coffee talks and management meetings inside HP, and in speeches to analysts and reporters outside. What's more, she constantly thanks the team, personally, real time, dropping in just to shake a hand, say thanks, or even give a hug!

Hmm. A CEO who cares about her company's soul and who understands the importance of positive deviance? Maybe it's time for our skunkworks to come out from under cover.

Chapter 6

SERVING THE FOUR BILLION

At this point in history, with Internet technology, with what's happening in the world, more is possible than even the wildest-eyed radicals among us can imagine in our wildest dreams. And relative to what is possible in this moment for the world, even the most radical of us are conservative.

I talk to the spirits and they to me through the hundreds of books I buy, borrow, and browse. When I am confused about what I think, or lonely with my thoughts, I amble through a bookstore or browse online, and find a new friend. My new friends provide clues about the next steps for me.

Several years before Carly's arrival, one of the books that moves me deeply is Alex Counts's *Give Us Credit,* the story of the microlending revolution and the Grameen Bank, Dr. Muhammad Yunus's dream—and successful business model —for putting poverty in the museum of history. Not until I read this book, often in tears, can I acknowledge the chronic depression that has plagued me since I first believed, according to the religious tradition of my childhood, "The poor will be with you always." I can see what this belief has cost me. And I can see the possibility of Yunus's dream; I can see a year, a world, with no starving children. I buy twenty-five copies out of my HP Labs budget and pass them around, certain that Grameen is in HP's future and we must start to build for it.

An economics Ph.D. from Vanderbilt University, Muhammad Yunus returned home to a newly independent but war-ravished Bangladesh in the 1970s determined to make a difference. Nothing he tried worked. Finally, using twenty-six dollars of his own money, he began what would become Grameen Bank, a bank for the poorest of the poor. To get a loan, borrowers had to prove they had no collateral. Over time, the model evolved to lending not to an individual, but to each member of a pod of five. The first person to get a loan is the poorest, as determined by the small group. After s/he has made three repayments, the second person gets their loan. They make three repayments and then the third gets a loan.

Twenty-seven years later, the Grameen Bank lends $500 million a year to two million of the poorest people on Earth—it loans its three billionth dollar in 2000. What's more, it has a whopping 96 percent return rate—significantly better than my bank is getting from people like me. Using their loans and the social infrastructure that results from the groups of five aggregating into associations of two hundred (and these groups aggregating yet again), the poor of Bangla-desh are lifting their families out of poverty for the first time in generations. They have, in fact, just helped venture capitalize their country's cell phone business.

The story of the Grameen Bank has turned upside down the way bankers think about banking and how aid agencies think about aid. Can it help turn upside down how businesses think about business?

I wonder, what would be the parallel paradigm shift for HP? What if our noncustomers became our biggest market? What do the poorest of the poor need and how can HP help to meet their needs? I am sure that somehow HP can partner with Grameen and provide business models, technology, and solutions to help realize the dream. I talk to everybody about it and a couple of people keep talking with me: my favorite partners in crimes against the status quo, Laurie Mittelstadt and Sri-nivas Sukumar.

Radical Stand

PUT A STAKE IN
THE GROUND

Through the kinds of miracles that occur when passion is the fuel, I get to meet Dr. Yunus in November 1997. He is a co-chair and I am a board member at the State of the World Forum. I get Sukumar to come to San Francisco on a Sunday morning to talk with Dr. Yunus about bandwidth and fiber optic networks and all the possibilities we can imagine. After a breakfast, a lunch, and hours of discussion together, I return to HP more inspired than ever to help us become stewards of the planet—and specifically to partner with Grameen Bank to bring technology to those who need and want it in Bangladesh.

This begins what will become a couple of years of monthly discussions among Alex Counts, the head of Grameen Foundation USA, my buddy Laurie Mittelstadt, and me about what we might be able to do together. Now, I know this is a little iffy. Here I am, still basically a personnel manager, not a business person and not a technologist, talking to Grameen Bank as if I am going to make HP do anything.

Radical Move

START A
CONVERSATION—
AND LISTEN!

But I do bring in others, including Sukumar; the division general managers who had attended our sustainability meeting, like Webb McKinney; and outstanding consultants like Janine Firpo. In good conscience, I must keep reminding Alex how improbable it looks that HP will ever partner with Grameen Bank. But he is willing to keep talking. So we do.

I begin to realize that social equity is a critical dimension of the planet's sustainability, and vice versa. The environmental and the social equity movements proceed separately, and sometimes at great odds with each other. If there are too many of us people on Earth, some would argue, then on a planetary scale, it would be a good thing for millions of us to die out. To figure out ways to save ourselves and each other just hastens the destruction of the planet.

However, the people making these arguments are not the ones about to die. Those who are about to die, and those working with and for them, argue that the "first" world, having destroyed life all over the planet to establish itself, has no right to impose any more rigid standards—or lack of them— on other developing countries.

Alex and Laurie and I keep talking. We talk about how to get hundreds of used computers to Bangladesh and we look at all the ways to source them. We look at all the business models that would provide incentive for corporations like HP to do it. Nothing works. It's very discouraging. Plus, the people in Bangladesh are making huge leaps of progress and they don't want old computers anyway, not even two-year-old computers. So we start looking at a computer-service paradigm where we would sell or lease them new equipment, and, with the revenue they would earn from using the computers, they would pay for them, service them, and replace them. That looks pretty good.

In the meantime, Jim Sheats, now the company's "technology for sustainability" guru, has scaled up from the HP
for Sustainability "customer visit" and is talking with the MIT Media Lab and the former
president of Costa Rica, Jose Maria Figueres,
about producing "Little Intelligent Communities" (LINCOS) to be dropped into remote
areas of Costa Rica.

Radical Tool

SCALE UP

LINCOS are basically "cyberkiosks."
The kiosk itself is a recycled shipping container—the kind
that is used on ships and airplanes but is too stressed out to
be used reliably for shipping anymore. The container gets
converted into a solar-powered porta-computer center with
computers, printers, and networking connections, and then
is dropped into the jungles and rainforests to enable rural
people to access the Internet and online health care, weather,
and other general information. Scaled up, such telecenters
could allow rural villages—where 60 percent of the world
lives—to leapfrog urbanization and the accompanying break-
down of family and community.

The plan is to produce fifty of these self-contained
cyberkiosks and have them be the model for wiring the developing world at very low cost: $100,000—and eventually
one-third of this—apiece. Lyle Hurst completely "gets" the
promise of this project and contributes the largest part of the
equipment for the first unit. He is the executive in the loop
who then, with Jim, partners with Figueres to produce more
cyberkiosks for Costa Rica as well as for the Dominican Republic.

In January of 2000, I am sitting in a meeting with Jim

about the cyberkiosks, trying to focus on what people are saying. Yesterday I was tentatively diagnosed with aggressive uterine cancer and I am going for more tests tomorrow, but my doctor had tears in his eyes when he told me that what he had discovered was not good and only surgery would tell. I am freaked out but haven't talked about it yet.

I look around the room and hear the voices and see the people sitting there without me. Only somehow I'm the air of the place. Or they are the waves and I've sunk back into the ocean. And for the first time in my life, I calmly get it that my own death is okay, it's insignificant, because everything I believe in will continue after I'm gone. My children will be carried along in this great ocean of possibility. I've read something recently about transpersonal psychology— the shift of ego identify from self to something bigger. Am I experiencing it?

I go on the required medical leave and prepare for the surgery. Sukumar calls me when he gets the news and after talking about life and death, he offers, "I'm going back to India to see my mom over the holiday and she doesn't live all that far from Bangladesh. Want me to see if I can meet with Muhammad Yunus again and follow up on our conversations?"

"Great," I say. "If Jim can make the time, I'll send him over, too, to see if they have any interest in cyberkiosks. I'll also contact these two guys in the field who have been trying to sell HP computers into Bangladesh without success— there's a big technology trade show coming up there where all the high-tech companies—including us—are going to give demos. Maybe you and Jim can connect with the local guys and help them out at the trade show after you meet with Dr. Yunus. Let's see what you guys can cook up."

Sukumar and Jim Sheats meet with Dr. Yunus, and he is not only interested in the concept of cyberkiosks, he wants them for Bangladesh. This is the start of the Grameen Telecenter Project. The trade show, too, turns out great. The HP demos go very well with Sukumar and Jim joining the local HP team there.

My feeling of elation about the Bangladesh project combines with the calm I felt earlier. I get through the medical tests, go over wills, reassure family and friends. The surgery proves the tumor benign and I recover splendidly. I feel better than I have in years.

So here I am in HP Labs: I'm still wrapping up my work as worldwide change manager, ramping down from the split off of Agilent Labs, helping Ron Crough transition into the new job, and helping with various skunkworks projects like Jim's.

We keep these skunkworks below the radar screen by keeping them small, or, as they grow, distributed across groups. Lyle and I now each have about half of the LINCOS business. But then, in spring of 2000, something amazing happens. Glenda Dasmalchi, one of our friends in Corporate Communications, calls to see if we have anything interesting going on. I send her to Jim, who tells her about the latest with LINCOS and with Grameen. And she tells Carly.

It turns out that Carly completely gets it and wants us to scale up and do real businesses here. Within weeks she signs agreements with Muhammad Yunus and Jose Maria

Figueres! After years of flying low, this is going so fast I am breathless with excitement.

Radical Tool

SCALE UP
EVEN MORE

Next, the Grameen folks are interviewed on video so Carly can explain HP's interest to a big meeting of analysts that she is addressing. Lyle briefs her on all that could happen with some full-time focus—he's helping with the telecenter projects on top of a more-than-full-time job as the vice president of our digital-media-solutions business. She is enthusiastic and asks him to make her a proposal for a full-scale business. He does this in record time and Carly asks him to lead it.

It's named "World e-Inclusion."

I'm thrilled. This is happening so fast and at such a scale it's hard to believe. Lyle is an incredible visionary on behalf of the poor, on behalf of HP's potential for making a difference, and on behalf of the business. He invites Jim Sheats and me to join him, and begins to hire the rest of the team. With deep and sophisticated understanding of the business and social agenda, and his own full support, the new vice president of HP Labs, Dick Lampman, lends me full time to Lyle's business. This allows me to stay close to HP Labs and troll constantly for technology and developments that bear on the new business, yet remain very involved in scaling this up into a thriving business.

World e-Inclusion is a virtual business, an Internet startup inside HP whose goal is to deliver the benefits of the Internet—that is, more choices in life based on better information—to the four billion at the bottom of the economic pyramid. At first, all our staff is borrowed, meaning they have to do their regular jobs some of the time and can work on World e-Inclusion the remainder of their time. We don't have a brick-and-mortar building, but we have so much energy and enthusiasm, it's no deterrent to be spread geographically across HP.

So what is my role in all this? I operate "three to four orbits out," as I put it, scouting for danger, opportunities, and resources for the business. I also feel that we urgently need to assemble a larger team to be our context, a team that has firsthand knowledge of the issues with which we will be dealing. I start recruiting people for an advisory board, using my network of friends and consultants working in the areas of social responsibility and the four billion. I also help Lyle to recruit our first staff.

I don't know what to call myself anymore. I'm all over the map, doing everything. People ask, "Are you the marketing manager of this new business? The sales manager? Are you Personnel? Alliances?" I explain the origins of the business and how I'm doing a little of everything. One of the people I talk to says, "Oh, you're a founder!" I try that out on Lyle and he says, "That's right!" My new business cards say "Co-Founder, World e-Inclusion."

Unbelievable.

We do benchmarking research that tells us that other big companies, like HP itself, are donating money to help the poor in the areas where they have factories or sales organizations. This is the *philanthropic* model: You give to the poor. But what Muhammad Yunus has done and what we aim to do is to create *self-sustaining, profit-making* businesses, so the rural poor can create better lives for themselves by relying on their own entrepreneurial skills and not charitable donations, which can suddenly dry up.

But can this new approach be profit making for the businesses who "target" this emerging market? Certainly the Grameen Bank is successful lending to the poor, but would there be enough profit to satisfy a multinational corporation?

The answer is yes. In their paper "Strategies for the Bottom of the Pyramid," submitted to the *Harvard Business Review,* renowned scholars and consultants C.K. Prahalad and Professor Stuart L. Hart call the four billion "the biggest potential market opportunity in the history of commerce."

This market, however, is invisible to the corporate world, they say, because it is generally regarded as hard to reach—in terms of communications, credit, and distribution. These are daunting drawbacks: If you can't tell the customer about your product, if the customer doesn't have the money to buy it, and if you can't easily deliver the product to the customer, why bother?

Prahalad and Hart have developed a model to address those issues and open this market for the benefit of both the poor and the multinational corporations.

"Contrary to popular assumptions," they write, "the poor can be a very profitable market—especially if MNCs [multinational corporations] are willing and able to change their business models. The bottom of the pyramid is not a market that allows for traditional (high) margins. Like the Internet space, the game is about volume and capital efficiency. Margins are likely to be very low (by current norms) but unit sales extremely high. Managers who focus on gross margins will miss the opportunity. Managers who innovate and focus on economic profit will be rewarded."

By solving the communication and distribution problems, it will be possible for the first time ever to create "a single, interconnected market uniting the world's rich and poor in the quest for a truly sustainable form of economic development."

Developing this market has four aspects. First is increasing the buying power of the poor. These new consumers must have access to credit and realistic opportunities to increase their income. Second, they must be educated on the importance of sustainability so that the market boom to come does not devastate the environment. Third, the products and services offered must be based on both advanced technology and local knowledge and practices. Finally, low-cost, high-quality, decentralized distribution systems must be devised.

"The Tier 4 [i.e., the bottom tier of the economic pyramid] opportunity is not restricted to businesses serving 'basic needs' such as food, textiles, and housing," Prahalad and Hart point out. "On the contrary, the bottom of the pyramid represents a massive opportunity for 'high-tech' businesses such as financial services, cellular phones, and low-end computers. In fact, for many emerging, disruptive technologies (e.g., fuel cells, wind energy, photovoltaics, satellite-based telecommunications), the bottom of the pyramid may prove to be the most attractive early market.

"In twenty years," Prahalad and Hart continue, "we may look back to see that Tier 4 provided the early market pull for the disruptive, new technologies which only later penetrated and replaced the unsustainable technologies in the developed markets of the world."

It's always nice when the experts confirm that you know what you're doing . . .

We put together a business plan focusing on the rural poor among the four billion to develop businesses and business models that enable them to make money and sustain anything we start together. That means, to sustain *economically* (through the money they make), to sustain *culturally* (through being in their language, in their village, and appropriate to their values), and to sustain *environmentally* (through offering mostly services, not stuff; and where there is stuff, making it small stuff, not big stuff). One such project might be an extension of the cyberkiosk: a full village-based computing center where people can go to do data-entry jobs, access telemedicine, get literacy and vocational training, and get access to markets for their crops or crafts.

We envision a woman in Bangladesh or the Dominican Republic who usually takes four or five eggs to the next town to sell every day. But if she can use the Internet to communicate with the kiosk in the next town and finds out they already have enough eggs, then she can go to a different town and sell her eggs—eggs that might not have gotten sold in the first village, where there was an oversupply. Then, with successful sales, she can get another hen. And she can grow her business, and grow it, and grow it.

And so can all the villagers. Somebody's selling eggs and somebody's selling woven goods and somebody's selling seeds and somebody's selling a goat. Farmers can use the Internet to get information about weather conditions so they can harvest before the rains come, or not go fishing when there's a storm expected. A mother with a high-risk pregnancy can be examined via ultrasound in her village and the images transmitted to the specialist hundreds of miles away. A father can click on pictures of the symptoms of his son's sickness and get a diagnosis online. And this is just the beginning.

We work with the Harvard School of Public Health and start scanning all the demographic data of the world to learn about the rural areas where the four billion live. We're not including urban areas because that's already happening, thanks to other people's efforts. It's the rural poor among the four billion who are left without resources. Besides, if we can improve the lives of the rural poor, they won't have to leave their homes, breaking up the rural infrastructure that supports them and moving to blighted cities that don't have culture or connections for them.

With Lyle's enthusiastic support, I track down an old friend from earlier days in HP and from the State of the World Forum, as well: James Moore of Harvard, the chairman of Geopartners Ventures, who was recognized by *Business Week* as one of the top three business consultants in the world today.

I think Jim's breakthrough methods for identifying business ecosystems and creating strategies for unbalancing them in favor of better futures for his clients are exactly what we need for the rural poor. What if we can somehow draw out who's playing in this emergent sector, which I call the social entrepreneurial sector (doing well by doing good), see how we're playing and where we're sub-optimizing, and look at what strategically placed 2 percent tweaks could allow for, for the poor and for HP?

I also ask Jim to help us "segment the market" for the rural poor, worldwide. After sharing a laugh at the seeming contradiction of applying the concept of market segmentation to what is traditionally seen as a social development problem, Jim suggests that we tap into the work of Amartya Sen, winner of the Nobel Prize in economics for his work on how societies build economic development while increasing personal freedom. The best way to accomplish this turns out to be connecting with the Program on Society and Health at the Harvard School of Public Health.

Working with Harvard, Jim starts in immediately and soon emerges as the chair of our international World e-Inclusion board. He begins to staff up the board with the most amazing luminaries representing knowledge of or skills critical for the rural poor.

Among the first:

- Barry Bloom, dean of the Harvard School of Public Health, one of the world's leading experts on health in the developing world. Barry brings a focus on public-health policy, technology, measurement, and education, with a special focus on the eradication of tuberculosis and malaria, a large part of the disease burden in the developing world.
- Sam Pitroda, chairman of WorldTel, which is chartered by the International Telecommunications Union to bring communications services to the developing world. He's the leader of India's telecom

revolution and of policies that have led India to become a world power in technology research and education. He's very interested in disseminating low-cost, widely available information and communications technologies, and in the technology to promote literacy and health education.

- To my great joy, my dear Joel Birnbaum joins the board as one of the world's information-technology research leaders, bringing his expertise at basic and applied research to address the challenge of completing one of his stated missions in life: to make information technology truly pervasive, and in this effort, scalable and relevant to the rural poor.

- Loung Ung, a Cambodian human rights activist and author of *First They Killed My Father*, a book about the realities of life and death under the Khmer Rouge. She campaigns for a land-mine-free world and brings deep knowledge of the needs of the rural and displaced poor.

- Hafsat Abiola from Nigeria, a twenty-four-year-old human rights organizer and dear friend. Her father, Moshood, won the presidential election held in Nigeria in 1993 but served out his term in solitary confinement, incarcerated by the military. He died in prison, on the eve of his release. Her mother, Kudirat, campaigning for his release, was assassinated in 1996 in the streets of Lagos. Hafsat established and directs an institute that promotes the development of women and youth as change-makers. She is also co-founder and first president of the International African Students Association, a Fetzer fellow, and a former fellow board member of the State of the World Forum.

In addition to supporting Jim with board development, I'm also scanning inside the company for other positive deviants, people or groups in HP who are already working in this area. It turns out we're doing a lot! It's just under the table, in the margins, tucked to the side.

Sitting in my office one day, because she needs a phone, is Cathelijne Grobbee, a Dutch HP employee, just back from Nigeria, where she has sponsored a conference. Soon she introduces me to her manager, Owen Kemp, and to Africa country sales manager Gerald Naidoo. They tell me about the technology institute we've created at the University of Ghana and the fifty banks that HP has helped open up in Africa in partnership with the World Bank, providing the necessary hardware, software, and e-services.

My colleague Betty Sproule, who's working on a project to track and catalyze all of the company's e-Inclusion activities, and I start connecting the dots. One role that's emerging for me is as an amplifier for everything already going on in this area that's aimed at the rural poor. I am also becoming one of the focal points for pulling these efforts together into one large, powerful arrow pointed at the target problem instead of a whole bunch of little weak ones.

Radical Tool

AMPLIFY
POSITIVE
DEVIANCE

More Scaling Up

Besides World e-Inclusion, another effort scales up to a

business from an idea originating at the Celebrations of Creativity.

Leslie Field, a scientist in HP Labs (later of Agilent Labs), and Rosanne Wyleczuk, a marketing resource and total inspiration in HP Labs, start what they playfully name

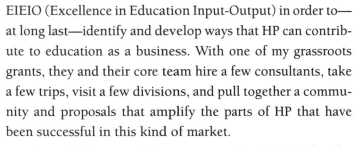

Radical Tool

SCALE UP

EIEIO (Excellence in Education Input-Output) in order to—at long last—identify and develop ways that HP can contribute to education as a business. With one of my grassroots grants, they and their core team hire a few consultants, take a few trips, visit a few divisions, and pull together a community and proposals that amplify the parts of HP that have been successful in this kind of market.

Soon their research becomes a project in HP Labs, developing the technologies for print-on-demand customized textbooks. Then the "e-School" project begins, its goal being to one day enable each elementary and secondary pupil in the U.S. (and eventually the world) to have a textbook tailored to his or her own strength, including learning style, preferred pace, and ease or difficulty in learning.

With Carly's sponsorship, the division projects work together, scaling up into the new e-Education business headed by Laura Cory, who, like Lyle Hurst, had early on been the behind-the-scenes senior management sponsor of this "world's best/best for the world" skunkworks.

It Takes Only One to Start

In the meantime, I talk to people in HP Labs about what I am doing. Support is immediate, energy electric. For example, I get a call from Tan Ha, a Vietnamese engineer who works upstairs and wants to come talk to me very urgently. I set up time with him.

When we sit down together, I can see he's feeling a lot. He says he has never talked to anyone about this before because it's not work related, but suddenly he sees how it could become work-related. Tan tells me he was a boat person—his body shakes as he describes the voyage. When he made it to the U.S., got an education, and found a good job, he used to look at his beautiful home and his healthy children and his good life, and ask, "Why me? Why did I live and the others die?" He had to do something to ease his guilt.

So Tan went back to Vietnam and found an orphanage run by nuns, with forty children ages five to eighteen that he started supporting along with some other now-successful boat people. "We send money and raise money—we raised $40,000 to help with the services required for the kids—but the kids never saw a penny. The money 'disappeared' before it arrived at the convent. Then we helped them get $140,000 to build a new building for the nuns who run the orphanage, and again the nuns never saw it.

"I want you to do something—I mean, I want World e-Inclusion to help. These *are* the poorest of the poor. These children are sleeping without clothes in freezing weather—in the mountains. I have seen them shivering."

I look at this brilliant engineer sitting across from me

Radical Tool

PLAY WITH
WHOEVER
SHOWS UP

Radical Stand

PUT A STAKE IN
THE GROUND

and feel my own tears rising. "Well, there are two things," I say to Tan. "One, I get very emotional about this too." Now we're both crying in the cafeteria. "And two, World e-Inclusion is not *they*, Tan. *They* are not going to do anything. *We* are going to do something.

"I want you to think about what you want to do and we'll help," I tell him.

"But this isn't my—"

"Just start talking about this passion of yours. It's no longer okay not to talk to anybody about it. We are going to make a list and you're going to walk away with it, then

Radical Move

START A
CONVERSATION—
AND LISTEN!

you're going to call me in on Friday and tell me whom you've talked to on the list. I want you to start with your lab director. Go to Stan Williams and tell him your dream."

"No, no, I have to read more about it. And I don't fully understand the economics of my country, and I don't understand exactly how orphanages—"

"You know enough. You know your dream. You can say you don't know what it means or what you're going to do about it, but you think it may have some relationship to HP. And leave it at that."

"Well, I don't know if I should go to Sta—"

"Look, Stan's favorite restaurant is the noodle house."

Tan perks up. "Which noodle house?"

"The one in the shopping center around the corner."

"Oh, that's a terrible noodle house! He shouldn't go there! I'll show him the best noodle house."

"You see, there you go. You go in there and talk with him about the noodle house and you'll have his attention."

Radical Move

TAP THE STRENGTH
OF YOUR
RELATIONSHIPS

Radical Move

BUILD YOUR
CADRE

I keep talking, but I think I've lost Tan. He's very private, always keeps work and personal stuff very separate. I say, "Okay, it's fine if you don't want to talk to Stan right away. Is there anyone Vietnamese you could talk to? Is there a Vietnamese Engineers Association?" Tan doesn't know. "Well, go ask Oanh Dang and Kiem Le; one of them will know. Because if there is such an association, and you were to tell them your dream, they'd probably donate and you would have a ton of money to just carry over in your pocket and hand to the nuns."

Tan comes up with a couple of names of other people who might help, and pretty soon we have a list of five people he can contact. I leave him with the list and get his promise that he'll call me in four days with the news that he has connected with one person.

Two days later, I get an e-mail from Tan's manager, Stan, saying, "I had a very interesting conversation with Tan this afternoon. I am very happy to sponsor him working directly for you 10 percent time on the orphanage in Vietnam. You know, we are working on molecular electronics, in the hope that it will provide massively cheap, very robust computing for the world. It will benefit our group to hear directly about the world into which we hope someday to contribute."

I write Tan and say, "See what happens when you start talking?" Stan Williams—who was recently on the front page of the *New York Times* and the *Wall Street Journal* because his group has created conductive wires only a few atoms

wide—a crucial part of building ultramicroscopic computers—completely "gets it."

Tan e-mails me back, "Do you think we should get the
United States ambassador to Vietnam involved?" I tell him it
might be a little soon for that.

But he may be right. I'm probably slowing him down.

Players in the Biggest Game

It's September 2000, two days before we finish the first
manuscript for this book. I'm helping to facilitate World e-
Inclusion's Discovery Session—a daylong meeting of fifteen
people, some with experience working with and for the rural
poor, and some from the new World e-Inclusion team. Many
on the team can't make it because they are working 'round
the clock on our World e-Inclusion business launch so that
the rest of us can attend.

I've left my consultant friend Rayona Sharpnack an urgent voice mail. I tell her I know I'm going to have to keep
my eye on the ball here, but could she please remind me
what the ball is? From the 2000 Summer Olympics in Sydney,
where's she watching the women's softball playoffs, she replies: "It's people's commitments. What they're on for. Keep
returning to these, because they create the playing field for
the biggest game."

The objective of today's conference is to vet the current
thinking of the team about the needs of the four billion, with
HP and outside field people working together to create a playing field on which we can successfully co-invent a new future for both the company and the rural poor.

Obviously what we create for the four billion are going

to have to be sustainable solutions. One aspect of "sustainable" is that it delivers value to everyone involved. In the case of HP and the small entrepreneurs who will be involved, the value is profit. For the customers on the ground, it is useful information and services. The solutions also have to be sustainable in the sense that even if we do provide a little philanthropy and consulting up front, it's got to be economically sustainable, as well as environmentally and culturally sustainable. These have to be solutions that reflect and preserve the best—as our new customers define it—in their own culture.

The day of the Discovery Session begins and I am very nervous: how to bring these two worlds together? Before the meeting even starts, I laugh at my fears when I see two of the participants in animated conversation: Jim Sheats, with ponytail, earrings, jeans, and combat boots, just back from Costa Rica; and Bob Hawkins, looking like a *GQ* ad, in shirt, tie, jacket, and dress shoes. Which one is the corporate guy and which from the nonprofit? I ask aloud, laughing. We all crack up. Jim is the HP guy; Bob the nonprofit guy, from the World Bank.

At times during this meeting, as I look around and listen to the attendees, I am moved to tears.

Hafsat Abiola is telling us of the two African boys, found frozen to death in the landing gear of a French airplane, and their letter to the world. It reads, in part, "Dear esteemed rulers in Europe, please help us in Africa. We are hungry and our parents are dead. You can help and we know you will if you only know of our situation." Hafsat says, "People always talk of the despair in Africa, the disease, wars, poverty. But they don't see the hope, the enormous hope, of the children and their faith that we will help them. This is what we must feel and allow it to guide us."

Christopher Shockey of HP, who is six-feet-seven-inches tall and who just cut off his ponytail, is an organic farmer. "There is no going back," he says. "I can't work for an HP or any other company that isn't going to be for the world. The bridges are burned behind me. This is our moment, this is our time. Now. I'm on. I'm on. Let's just do it."

My dear co-conspirator of the last twelve years, engineer Laurie Mittelstadt, is all lit up. She got it years ago that HP Labs needed to be best *for* the world, not *in* the world; and she went with me where no woman or man had gone before, to scale this vision up to the company and now the global level. She is talking about the alternative power sources she lies awake nights to invent, power that will cost the poor almost nothing, yet be rugged, reliable, and cheap.

Dennis Muscato of HP for years has considered his real work to be the volunteer work he and his wife do, taking used medical equipment to countries that lack it. Working at HP, he says, brings him enough income that he can afford to be involved in this effort without pay.

Jerry Sternin of Save the Children, fresh off the plane from Myanmar, is brainstorming collaborations between HP and his organization, and dreaming aloud of what HP could mean to the poor people with whom he lives and works. Suddenly, we are seeing new businesses as Jerry, eyes twinkling, paints a picture of HP collaborating on: an Internet-enabled training project for human-rights workers, called "Human Potential"; an Internet business in the service of nonprofits, called "HP³: HP Helping Partners Help People"; and AIDS education around the world, "HIV Prevention."

Gabrielle Villa, who was recruited from executive communication into World e-Inclusion just as she was considering joining the Peace Corps so she could do more meaningful work for the world, now believes she can do that work within HP, which is why she has decided to stay.

Janine Firpo, former marketing manager at Apple and now an Internet consultant to the poor around the world, is urging us on. "We can't begin to co-invent appropriate solutions for the rural poor until we live with them, sleeping on the mud floor, walking ten miles for the morning water with our hostess who trudges along with a child on her back, a child in her belly, and a third child tugging at her leg." The rural poor are enormously creative, she points out, rich with ideas, insights, and initiatives. After all, they have learned to survive and feed their families in the harshest conditions in the world.

Lyle Hurst, our visionary leader, focuses intently on what each of us is saying, pushing us to dream bigger and be bolder, but also to focus, because this is our chance to demonstrate the commercial viability of tackling and solving the world's big problems. He says he's inspired by our CEO, who has assured him, "These problems are very, very hard. That's why no one has solved them. That's why HP should take them on."

Marie Therese Tong, our first employee in World e-Inclusion, a Singaporean and former IBM marketing manager, tells of her two years in Nepal teaching English to young women in Nepal, helping to build their self-confidence—and in the process gaining so much more than she gave. She recounts the generosity of her host family on one of her trips out to the village, who insisted she have the straw mat on the dirt floor on which they all usually slept, and put it in the warmest corner of their straw hut. She recalls how warm and cared for she felt, despite the cold outside. And she imagines what the Internet and relevant information, HP, and all of us can do for the people of our world.

Gita Gopal, an HP Labs engineer, is just back from India, where she previewed possible technology for village communications. For months afterward, her extended family will send her newspaper stories containing quotes from her interviews with the Indian press.

Bob Haskell from the World Bank's World Links for Development talks with great excitement about how he and some friends formed this group inside the bank as a skunkworks. He tells us how successful it's been in making a difference for people, putting computers in Uganda and Palestine, and teaching teachers how to use the technology to supplement their meager curricula.

Tan Ha, our HP Labs engineer, tells us in intense, rapid-fire speech that he's leaving in a week for Vietnam. He has networked all over the company and throughout Silicon Valley with other Vietnamese, and will be meeting with people in Hanoi and Saigon to explore business collaborations to benefit the poor of his country, beginning with financial software that will enable the huge Vietnamese-American community here to send money back to Vietnam to help— e-money that will actually arrive at the doors of the people who are being sent funds by their family in the diaspora, money that doesn't totally disappear before it gets there.

Bill Dwyer, my co-facilitator, a veteran of almost three decades at HP, is one of the few HP people at the meeting who looks like what we're "supposed" to look like. Bill has had experience in many functions, technologies, and businesses. Red-eyed from lack of sleep after days of travel, he's donating this day out of his tightly budgeted time because, "We must do the things that matter. This is what we must do."

And I suddenly see that the "company" is those with whom we break bread—the ancient meaning of the word, or as the Swedish word for business has it, "that which nourishes." The names of the companies and agencies and organizations on all our different business cards are just the distribution channels and tools for the miracles that lie ahead.

This is our moment. This is our time. I'm on. I'm on. Let's do it.

A week later, on October 16, 2000, we launch World e-Inclusion at the "Creating Digital Dividends" conference in Seattle, sponsored by the World Resources Institute. The goal of this summit is for the participating companies, nonprofits, and governmental organizations to consider the future of the world and what digital technology has to offer.

CEO Carly Fiorina keynotes the conference and announces our vision for providing all people with access to social and economic opportunities. She pledges that in 2001, HP's new business will touch one thousand villages across the world through "initiatives that provide measurable social and economic benefits" to the rural poor. Our new business will also enlist one million partners in the initiative, ranging from major alliances and global partners to regional organizations, local project teams, and individuals. Finally, she says, World e-Inclusion is targeting $1 billion of HP and partner products and services to be sold, leased, or donated in 2001 through special e-Inclusion programs.

Immediate press coverage of the launch appears in the *New York Times*, the *Wall Street Journal*, *Information Week*, the *Dow Jones Business News*, and on CNN. Global coverage follows.

And so goes the fabulous kickoff of the biggest game yet on the infinite playing field, "Soul in the Computer."

Chapter 7

AND IN THE END...

There was a time when you were not a slave, remember that. You walked alone, full of laughter, you bathed bare-bellied. You say you have lost all recollection of it. . . . You say there are no words to describe this time, you say it does not exist. But remember. Make an effort to remember. Or, failing that, invent.
—Monique Wittig, *Les Guérillères*

So far this book has been saying, here's how we can come out of our resignation and unconsciousness: Here's how we do it at the group level, and here's how to begin to do it at the company and global level. Now, I know that appreciating Rolf Jaeger's music is not going to stop corporate exploitation, but once we wake up to the whole person in each other we can keep each other conscious and inspired so that we *can* change things. We can take the next step.

The next step is to achieve a responsible globalization. Thinking on paper, here is my working definition of that term.

As usual when I'm beginning to define something, I remember a story that embeds the soon-to-be-realized principles I'm grappling to understand . . .

It's the early '70s and I'm writing a feminist newspaper column for the newspaper in Madison, Wisconsin. As a result, I have become sort of a community ombudsman for issues around sexism, violence against women, and the like. One morning a woman I'll call Mimi phones and asks to meet with me. She is a small, pretty woman in a pink shirtwaist, with perfect hair.

Mimi tells me she is part of a professional association that is having its annual meeting in Madison and the only woman on the entire agenda is Miss Dairymaid Wisconsin. She is very upset. "It's terrible. There are so many good women we could be having, but it's too late. I don't know what to do. I'm beside myself, I'm so angry. I want to march or protest or do something but I can't think of what!"

I can't imagine how I can help her, but as sometimes occurs, I notice I've left my body and am looking down on us both from the back corner of the restaurant. To my surprise I hear myself say, "You're not going to march. You're going to stay inside the meeting and keep wearing that pink dress. But I'm going to call my friends in the radical women's group to march on the first day of your conference. And I'll call my friends at the newspaper and the two TV stations to cover the march.

"That's going to pressure the conference organizers to respond—and they will have no idea what to say. You will. That's when you'll hand them a list of women whom they're going to invite as speakers next year."

When the big day arrives, the students come out and march. It's the early '70s so my protester friends have unshaved legs, hairy armpits—the whole deal. The newspaper and TV friends look their part and are there covering things. Inside, the association president is having an apoplectic fit because this is a "professional" group and he wants to keep it that way. He's running around asking his conference staff, "What am I going to say to these protesters?"

At which point Mimi in her pink dress pops up and says, "You can tell them it was an oversight and it won't happen again. Tell them we have a list of women candidates for next year and half of the speakers will be women. Here's a list you can use."

He is so relieved to have the list, he is quite happy to commit to it. So out he goes and makes the announcement. The march and the president make the evening news. And sure enough, next year the speakers are fifty-fifty men and women . . .

The point of this story? That it takes all of us, each doing our part, working together, inside and out, to bring about the change we need. Had Mimi left the inside to go out and protest, she could never have done as good a job as the folks already out there. Had they only protested—and they would never have known to protest this event had Mimi not told me and I told them—there would have been no one inside with the list in hand that became the step forward for the next year. Endless arguments about who is more politically correct, Mimi or the protesters, just wastes precious energy that could be spent on doing the hard work of change.

What if the globalization issues could scale up? And what if everyone had a role, and we worked together? The protesters, either organized or as individual citizens, would amplify the negative and call for change, thus producing external pressure. This would create an opening for the people inside the corporation whose values are in alignment with those of the protesters. These "insiders" would then amplify the positive (or use some other revolutionary tool) to effect change from within.

To take it one step further, the people inside a given corporation can connect with like-minded people inside other corporations, who then use "competitive analysis" to say, "Hey, look what they did. We should do better than that or we'll be left behind!" Then you let your friends in the other company know what you've done, and they go back and point to it in their competitive analysis and escalate to the next level of change. In this way we can consciously evolve the whole corporate sector, each company leapfrogging the next. This strategy is already working.

But if the people demonstrating in the streets are sneering at Mimi because she shaves her legs, wears pink dresses, and belongs to the "offending" organization, or if Mimi is totally appalled by the protesters, we lose the possibility of radical change.

In the opening chapter, I shared the story of my colleague who got the organic farmer who works on our World e-Inclusion team jeered out of an organic farming conference when he told the other participants that he worked for a corporation. Dividing ourselves into "us" and "them" will make it harder—or perhaps impossible—to change the corporate behaviors that hurt the world and to grow the behaviors that help. If we divide, those behaviors will conquer. There is no longer time for this luxury, for long.

The domestic-partners incident is a good example of grassroots action (the action being conversation in this case) both inside and outside the company sparking a conversation inside the company that results in decisions being reversed at the executive level. I know this is possible around some of the globalization issues. Conversations, I can promise, are already going on inside our companies among people who care about these things with the people who will make the decisions—in some cases they are the same people. Attend any meeting of Business for Social Responsibility or the Social Venture Network if you have any doubt about this.

In addition to the protesters and the corporate revolutionaries, there's a third role that needs to be played in order to effect large-scale change: media that chronicle our progress over time. The latter are not necessarily sympathizers. They are reporters who cover the initial event and its short-term (and positive, we hope) results for TV, newspapers, and Webcasts. This is crucial. We need the media to reflect back to us what's happening, to chart (and amplify) our progress. Otherwise our accomplishments go unnoticed and unappreciated by people outside the cause—and even inside the cause. People who must remain committed over the long haul and new people who might be motivated to work for change in their organizations were they to hear about our successes all lose out, and consequently the world loses.

The media's role also needs to include reporting what's happening on the macro level. For example, when a business magnate donates millions to a nonprofit, there may be an article in the newspaper. Ditto when a group like the Packard Foundation provides billions in grants to good causes. But the larger issue—in this case, corporate profits being plowed back into the common good—isn't getting tracked. It's easy to see why: It's often not until the second, third, or fourth derivative of a positive action that its most powerful effects are visible. If you're not tracking the results of the initial action over time, you don't know about the larger effect.

This kind of reporting would help the for-the-world movement today scale up from individual companies like HP to the corporate-sector level. Scaling up is important because if more companies don't join us, we're not going to be able to transform *any* of our companies. Without some sort of unity, no corporation is going to find a way to face down Wall Street.

Wall Street is basically the boss right now. It gives us a quarterly report card, and you can't get too many bad report cards before you're fired as the CEO. So how do you balance the demand for short-term financial gains with the reality that for-the-world programs may or may not result in long-term financial gains? Those programs require an investment that's going to look like a loss on the quarterly report card, even though the possibility of their long-term profitability is proven.

Having said all this, I also have to say that I don't know exactly how we're going to create globalization "for the world." But I know that we can and I know that we must. Maybe where we start is by finding where we want to work— outside or inside the corporation—and just work it.

Doing this may take us into territory we're not comfortable with, but personal growth is often painful—and the only alternative is slow death. I always believed that to get up in front of a large group and talk to lots of people, you had to be an extrovert. You couldn't be shy like me. (I would rather be in bed reading a book than almost anything else.) But because people have heard about our adventures at HP, I get asked to speak. To large groups. Terrifying! What do I do?

Just as in the years when I did very little stepping out

because I hate it so much, I stop sleeping for nights ahead of time, I write and rewrite everything I'm going to say and every candid remark I might make, and I get nauseated right before I go on stage. Unlike the earlier years, I keep on going because I remember Who I work for. I scale up and go to the largest context. I remind myself how much I want to accomplish my dream of HP raising the standard on corporate citizenship, on how we treat each other in the work environment, how we treat our customers, and how we treat the world. I remind myself that to move this dream along, I need to step out, speak up, take a stand.

So I automatically say yes when somebody asks me to speak. I don't think about it. There's no point. I am an introvert and I hate speaking in public, so if I think about it, I'll say no. Coming from my deep commitment to social change and sustainability, though, I have to speak—to be listened into speech—to recruit co-conspirators, and all the rest of it.

The bottom line is, when I come from my commitment, I'll do these risky things, even though the fear doesn't go away.

So I step out, even though I'm shy, even though I don't really know what I'm doing. If I wait till I'm comfortable that I do know what I'm doing, I've wasted precious time—and missed the opportunity to be taught by all who come forward to help me learn because they can see I'm bumbling around. On many levels, I have no business talking about globalization. I don't know enough. But that's just the problem—many of us who could be helping don't know enough. So we do nothing. This, I believe, is worse, albeit more comfortable (in the short term). So let's talk and move this conversation along. We'll learn whatever else we need to know as we go. But go we must.

We have to do something about our precious, suffering world. The land is suffering, the poor are suffering, the air and water and children and trees are suffering, even the rich are suffering. We seem to be going to hell in a handbasket at record speed. We can choose to default to that, or we can envision an alternative, create it, and live for our dream.

I've discovered something very surprising about having a dream. Our culture tells us in many ways that it's easy to know what we want, but it's hard to get it. That knowing what we want takes only a split second but getting it will take our whole life. And, oh, by the way, once we get it, we die. This is the view of the world we get from such classics of Western culture as Jason and the Golden Fleece, the search for the Holy Grail, and *Star Wars*. All these guys know what they're looking for, it takes them forever to find it, and then they die.

How my life actually works, though, is like this: The thing that takes the longest for me is coming out of unconsciousness long enough or often enough to discover what I want. This can take years. Once I know what my dream is, although there may be obstacles—even great ones—they melt away in the face of strong desire. I get what I'm going for. Time and time again. And I haven't died yet.

Just the opposite, in fact.

Somehow in the course of my journey at HP, what I am about got bigger, more pervasive. I tried a lot of different things in a lot of different settings, and got to see them all coming together. In terms of impact, I have scaled up. At

Santa Clara Division I was doing my dream at the division level. When I got to Corporate, I was doing it at a company level. Now my job at HP has me looking at creating positive, humanistic change on a global scale.

And I'm still scared. And I'm still going to do it. Me and my co-conspirators, inside and outside the corporation. Want to come along?

I hear often in my dreams the words spoken in a feminist play I performed in San Francisco almost thirty years ago: "There was a time when you were not a slave . . . remember . . . remember . . . remember. Or, failing that, invent." Then I felt it for women. Now I feel it for the world.

Chapter 8

TOOLS FOR REVOLUTIONARIES

There's this Chinese bamboo. You plant the seed, you wait. Nothing seems to happen. You wait some more. Still nothing seems to happen. This goes on for four years. In the fifth year, the thing shoots up eighty feet! I think a lot of our change efforts and a lot of what we stand for feels like this: insignificant, nothing is happening. But here's the deal: We have to believe that we are the bamboo under the ground, and we are going to shoot up eighty feet one day and the barren desert will become a bamboo forest.

*S*ome gardeners are very organized. In their corner of the garage, they have the small tools in one bin, the shovels and hoes in another, the gardening gloves and knee pads on their special shelf. Other gardeners are like me—I probably have ten trowels because I can't ever find one.

And without friends like Rayona Sharpnack—a wonderful external consultant who has helped me put what I know into words and has been a model for some of the key tools in my collection—I'd have no garage at all. I'd still be doing by blind instinct what I now can talk about clearly and share with others. Through Rayona, I meet Margot Silk Forrest, who not only sorts all the puzzle pieces of my life, talks, and memories, but organizes them into clearly labeled bins of "garden tools."

What I'm going to give you in this chapter is an organized set of tools, but don't let their order confuse you. At any given point, what you need to use may be a combination of step 1 and tool 4, or some new tool you'll create by combining two of them. In fact, you may never do steps 1, 2, and 3 in order.

So while this chapter is neat and orderly, life isn't. Use any of these tools whenever and wherever you need them. Give them better names, share them with others, invent new ones.

Here's an overview of what's in my corner of the garage, when it's neat and orderly (which is how they always start out).

Step 1.
RADICAL STAND: PUT A STAKE IN THE GROUND
- Remember Who You Work For
- Commit
- Keep the Faith
- Be the Change You Want to See

Step 2.
RADICAL MOVE: RECRUIT CO-CONSPIRATORS
- Tap the Strength of Your Relationships
- Start a Conversation—and Listen!
- Build Your Cadre

Step 3.
RADICAL TOOLS: USE THE RIGHT TOOL
- Scale Up, Scale Down

- Amplify Positive Deviance
- Turn "Enemies" into Allies
- Reframe the Context of What You're Doing
- Go to a Larger Context
- Play with Whoever Shows Up
- Tweak, Don't Toss
- Hold Up a Mirror

Sounds straightforward. But the ten steps or twelve principles or fifteen perspectives for a great life or a clean house or a terrific team have never worked for me. Life is messy. And to further complicate things, as I discovered, created, and collected these tools, they stopped being individual techniques and became more of an ecosystem. They run into each other, one leading to the next, to the next, and back to the first—in whatever order you find you reach for them.

The project to make HP Labs the "world's best" shows the messiness of life and the overlap between the tools:

We start out by putting a stake in the ground: The reason we are going to become the best for the world is because we say so. We care about it and we commit to it.

Next, we have to admit that we don't know what being "world's best" means, so we ask questions, we start a conversation. We decide to do this by adapting the existing employee survey to our use (tweak, don't toss).

When the reams of results come in, we listen to what each person says. Then we communicate the re-

sults to management by holding up a mirror using Readers' Theater. Senior managers "get" the problem and become co-conspirators in changing the things that are preventing us from being "best," as now defined by folks across HP Labs. They are doing what wants to be done.

The first thing they do is to develop their Hoshin-Lite plans. They are no longer "the bosses" telling the next level what to do; they are working on their own arenas. These particular "enemies" have turned into allies.

They also give me a budget. I make the budget available to anyone with an idea, and listen as person after person comes in to tell me about their dreams. I play with whoever shows up. I encourage their ideas. I suspend judgment, and I get them the resources they need—money from my grassroots grants budget or connections to others who can help—to take the first steps. (Whenever I get doubts about this whole process—some of the ideas, at first hearing, seem to make no sense—I remember Who I work for.)

Thus, what started as a conversation between the person with the idea and me has scaled up into a relationship. And their dream has scaled up into an actual project that they have the resources to pursue. These folks want to change the status quo (the state of not being the world's best); they are positive deviants, and by funding them, I have started amplifying them.

And that was only the first year of the project, before any of the grassroots initiatives produced results!

The more you use these tools, the more you will use these tools. Like me, you will use them in your personal life as well as your work life, and the world will become an infinitely richer place to live.

Step 1: Put a Stake in the Ground

We hear about this problem in the world, that bright idea in some company, this other person who has succeeded or failed to make a difference, and we think, *That's a shame*, or *That's interesting*. And we proceed with our day.

Then we hear about something else. Something that hits too close to home, or is too important to ignore, or is such a great idea we can't resist getting behind it. And we say, without thinking, "Hey, that's not okay!" or "Hey, I want to be a part of that!" or "Hey, I've got to help change that!"

In that moment, we've just put a stake in the ground. We now have a sense of agency in the world, a sense that we can make a difference. We forget whether we feel like an insider or an outsider and just take a stand about something that we personally believe in. It feels like a great danger *and* a great opportunity—in Chinese, the characters for these two words form the ideogram for "crisis." And

Radical Stand

PUT A STAKE IN
THE GROUND

in fact, it is a big danger—to the status quo: to who we've been and what the world has been until now. It's also a great opportunity, for our own future and for the future of the world.

When we put a stake in the ground, suddenly things

open up. There may be no evidence that we can achieve what we set our minds and hearts on, but when we take a stand, evidence starts popping up everywhere. Life starts collaborating with us.

I was depressed most of my life before I learned to put a stake in the ground. My religion told me "the poor will always be with you," and as an adult some part of me was resigned to the hopelessness of it, even though I tried to make a difference. Now, *trying* to make a difference when you and even your religion hold that it's hopeless is not putting a stake in the ground the way I mean it. My activity to end poverty when I believed it was hopeless led me to depression, martyrdom, and burnout.

Putting a stake in the ground requires commitment to change things. Not *trying* to change things—trying is poking at the situation—but *committing* to doing whatever it takes to change the situation. If I didn't have a stake—or, in my case, two or three—in the ground, I would still be depressed. Instead, I'm exhilarated, often exhausted, but almost never depressed!

I believe that a lot of the depression that we in the "developed" countries suffer is our deep knowing about the pain of the rest of the human family, our hopelessness over making any difference about it, and our guilt that by any measure, we've got more than our fair share. It's an awful cycle. I believe that as more of us put stakes in the ground, fewer of us will be depressed.

We'll wake up to the planet and what's going on around us. We'll be open to the possibility that we can make a difference. Because I have a stake in the ground on behalf of women and children living in poverty, I knew who Muhammad Yunus of Grameen Bank was when he crossed my path; I had read a book about him. Without my stake in the ground, he wouldn't even have been on my radar screen. Instead, he's not only my hero, but a business partner with my company.

REMEMBER WHO YOU WORK FOR

Stake in the ground or not, there are times when our courage or confidence flags. Times when the naysayers—including the loudest ones, the ones in our own heads—seem to be winning. When the small-minded, short-term path is so much easier to take than the big-minded, long-term one.

Radical Stand

REMEMBER WHO
YOU WORK FOR

This is when I have to remember Who I work for.

I feel that our real boss has to be whatever we think the Higher Power is. Whether it's God or nature or the Great Spirit, or it's some vision of a world that works for everyone, that's got to be our primary relationship. Because if it's anything smaller, we're going to go crazy with the personality conflicts, the politics, our own and others' pettiness—and we'll suboptimize all over the place.

In a way, remembering Who we work for is going to the largest context—and we scale up to it, ironically, by listening to "the still small voice within."

COMMIT

We hear a lot these days about working with passion and doing things with passion. Well, passion is great, but commitment is better. Commitment gets us through the eighteen-hour days, over the inevitable obstacles, and around the roadblocks that others (and we ourselves) throw up to stop us. My commitments get me up in the morning even though I don't feel like it, even though it seems hopeless. My commitments carry me through the troughs. If my commitments could speak, they would say, "I've put a stake in the ground and that's what I stand for and that's what I'm going to do, damn it!"

Radical Stand

COMMIT

Commitment, our intention to achieve huge, magnificent things in the world, will overcome any doubts we have that we can make a difference. Commitment outlasts passion; it does not come and go. It *includes* the "go."

Radical Stand

KEEP THE FAITH

KEEP THE FAITH

Putting—and keeping—a stake in the ground requires that we ride the waves of three traditionally uncomfortable seas: not knowing all the answers, running into obstacles, and not seeing immediate results.

Although these may seem like bad things, each carries its own gift.

1. Be Willing Not to Know

In our culture, the person who "has all the answers" is the one who gets respect. But what's more powerful? An answer? Or a question? One of my friends, generative consultant Ed Gurowitz, said to me once, "The greater the resolution of your proposal, the less room in it for other people to play."

He's right. I used to wait until I had fully thought out an idea and all its ramifications before I shared it with anyone. I learned this art in the academic world. It discourages stealing. The problem is, though, that when I did share my great ideas, mostly, nobody wanted to hear about them. The project was already fully formed; there was no room for anyone else's ideas. In fact, in academia, that's the point. Now I share ideas as soon as they pop into my head, and lots of people want to play, and everything scales up much faster. Of course, the "winning idea" may not have my name on it—in fact, it usually doesn't—but so much more gets done on behalf of the world I want to leave my children!

I love Zen master Suzuki Roshi's statement in *Zen Mind, Beginner's Mind*: "In the beginner's mind there are many possibilities; in the expert's mind there are few." Beginner's mind—the mind of someone who is willing not to know— is empty, open, available, and sharing. An expert's mind is already full, complete, needing nothing, and solid, like a block.

We have to get over our fear of not having the answers. If Joel Birnbaum had declared what would make HP Labs the best industrial research lab in the world, we would never have asked the people who worked there, the people who knew exactly what was keeping us from achieving "best." And in the fall of 2000, Joel wins the IEEE award for being the smartest man on the planet, or as they put it, for "outstanding engineering leadership."

2. Use Obstacles as Information

No matter how firm our will, how "righteous" our cause, we're going to run into obstacles. That's a given. In fact, we should *want* to run into them. Now, I know this and still I hate obstacles. But the fact is, no course of action is perfect at its conception. It's only by taking steps that we discover what works and what doesn't.

Obstacles are a gift because they provide us with information about the route we've chosen. They are feedback that tell us how to alter our approach, even our goal.

In the mechanical model, we avoid the things that would keep us from reaching our goal. But in a living system, we are open to the possibility that the "obstacles" are in fact the next task, even the next goal.

That's why we have to assume that resistance is a valid response. It's going to tell us something about our vision, what we're doing, or how we're doing it. There's information locked up in that resistance, and if we can explore it, we will learn very important things for reaching our goal.

In fact, my biggest human obstacles often turn out to be my best partners because of what they know that I don't know. I just have to learn to listen to them, not avoid them or turn them off.

3. Have Faith in Exponential Growth and Use the Right Metrics to Capture It

So we've put our stake in the ground, gathered some co-conspirators, and are off and running. But nothing seems to be happening. Nothing revolutionary, anyway. What's wrong?

Nothing. This is the process. Sudden growth isn't a characteristic of living systems, but exponential growth is.

Exponential growth is when not much appears to happen at first, or at second, or even at third—and then BOOM! Huge growth (or change) is visible. It's like a pond with a lotus in it. With each cycle, the number of lotuses doubles. That looks insignificant at first, but suddenly, in one cycle, the pond will go from half empty to completely full.

It's like that in a living-systems change process, such as the one we went through around being the "world's best." At first you think you are doing isolated, unrelated things that don't matter, because you can't see the patterns, the emerging harmonics, and you can't feel that it's an exponential phenomenon. There's no movie music or lighting change to let you know when you've turned the corner into a new phase, or just had the most significant conversation of the year. Underneath everything, though, is a force for growth that we don't know is working. We don't know it's going to take off until it does, but we have to have faith that it will.

When our HP Labs effort to be "world's best" started, Chandrakant Patel noticed that our engineers weren't talking to each other. They met at the coffeepot, but they didn't even say hi. So he started chalk talks. Friday afternoons, he'd reserve a room, and you could volunteer to be the person giving the chalk talk. Well, at the end of a couple of years, he'd had thirty-six chalk talks, each one of which could have been followed through to see what that led to, because technologies came out of them as people would cross-pollinate each other's ideas. But after two years, he was tired of it. He wrote his report, and was done with it.

In a Newtonian world, that would have been that. Cause: chalk talks; Effect: good conversations in the room, people talking to each other at the coffee pots now, some offline technology inventions.

But this was a living system. And what happened next was, Chandrakant said to himself, "Gee, it wasn't so hard to create these gatherings inside HP Labs. I think I'm going to do it for the company. I want to get together everybody who cares about thermal cooling inside computers." He knew only about six people who were interested, but each of them knew another six, and eventually ninety people showed up to his first thermal cooling meeting.

As of this writing, there have been four annual thermal-cooling conferences. Out of Chandrakant's experience of getting people together for chalk talks came a community that developed a whole new method of technology creation and transfer, and, out of that, a technology that is now the differentiator in HP's high-end servers. It has brought tens of millions of dollars of profit to the company.

We've seen this again and again. It isn't until the second, third, or even fourth derivative of many of our change efforts that the results to the bottom line show up. So if you don't use metrics that account for two or three derivatives out, you're not going to be able to prove to senior management—or even more important, to yourself—why this ought to be going on. Mechanical metrics of cause and effect miss the whole miracle.

Remember the story of the Chinese bamboo that does (apparently) nothing for one, two, three, four years? Then in the fifth year, it breaks through the ground and spurts eighty feet high. That's four times higher than the Olympic record for the pole vault.

The gift of exponential growth comes only if you don't leave before the miracle happens.

By the way, chalk talks are back and drawing a large crowd. That's another beauty of a living system: When something good goes away, people often realize that it is missing and want it back.

BE THE CHANGE YOU WANT TO SEE

Change starts with us. If we care about the sustainability of our planet, we recycle our newspapers and aluminum cans. If we want our corporations to care about sustainability, we model that at work. We walk our talk.

Radical Stand

BE THE CHANGE
YOU WANT TO SEE

If we want people to take more risks, to talk about the things we care about, then that's what *we* do. We act in accordance with the stake we have put in the ground. Gandhi said, "Be the change you want to see." A corollary to this principle is "bring the whole person to work." For me, this means using my radical past in the service of the present, not hiding it: introducing Readers' Theater to the corporate sector, speaking up against support of a bill that would cut funding for poor mothers and children, remembering Who I work for. If not me, then who? If not now, then when?

Bringing the whole person to work also means inviting others to do so. Like when we created a theme-park-type diorama of a doctor's office to present the vision of HP as a medical-technology company. We involved the whole person of the executives seeing our presentation. We invited the kid in them to get excited, to play with the idea. It brought them alive!

Our companies can't be whole until whole people come to work. And the world won't be whole until the companies are.

Radical Move

RECRUIT CO-CONSPIRATORS

Step 2: Recruit Co-Conspirators

As I said in the introduction to this book, every single thing I've done at HP has been in collaboration with somebody just as fired up as I was about it. I couldn't have done it alone. You can't either.

TAP THE STRENGTH OF YOUR RELATIONSHIPS

This is the secret of making things happen: *Multiply yourself.* Get the help, advice, and resources of people who care about you and/or the things you care about. These people are already your co-conspirators; work together!

Without my personal and professional relationships inside and outside of the company, virtually none of the things in my life would have been accomplished. At HP, no increase in minority recruiting, no domestic-partner benefits, no "world's best," no World e-Inclusion.

HP itself is a good example of the power of relationships. It was founded on a relationship of love and respect between two people. This is not the Hewlett company or the Packard company, but the Hewlett-Packard company. The order was decided not by higher or lower, greater or lesser, but by the flip of a coin. And the company grew through hundreds of significant relationships. Not just relationships with peers, but relationships up and down the hierarchy.

Look around you and talk to someone. Like Tan Ha, you may think you don't know anyone who can help you with your dream. Keep talking. Talk some more. Before you know it, you will have turned yourself into a movement!

START A CONVERSATION—AND LISTEN!

Recruit new co-conspirators. Start conversations. We ask someone a question: What do you think about this issue? Have you run into this before? What did you do then? Then we suspend judgment and *listen*. No matter how dumb or boring or predictable their response might sound to us at first, we encourage their ideas. We say, "Great idea!" And we listen some more.

We cannot make or keep good relationships unless we listen. And listen wholly, without preparing the next remark, without thinking about getting gas on the way home or whether our child did well on her math quiz. We must shut off the incessant judgment machine urging us to decide who's smarter, right, most likely to succeed. We must fall into each others' eyes.

When we do this, magical things happen. Things far greater than we could have imagined. Noncritical listening has the power to pull innovative ideas out of people. It's as if they were just waiting for someone to whom they could pour out their creative ideas.

Theologian Nelle Morton said thirty years ago, "In the beginning was not the Word but the Listening." That has proved itself true in my life. When I am sharing my ideas with someone, my experience is clear: Without my listener, I would not be having these thoughts. She or he is half the equation. I tried writing this book nine times—alone. Not until I recruited Margot Silk Forrest as my co-author could the dream of writing this book come true. Margot listened me into greater clarity, put together the points from my many talks and articles and our conversations into patterns I had only dimly discerned. Only then was there a book.

Traditionally, our culture has not noticed listeners, or rewarded us, or ranked us highly. Nor have we valued ourselves in this role. I completely undervalue my own role as a listener, and it took three conversations to convince Margot that, in fact, she is my co-author. Usually, she's not even mentioned in the books she works on with others! This has got to change.

Next time someone starts to share something with you—an idea, a feeling, even an anecdote, try this: Listen consciously, avidly, without a hint of judgment. Don't interrupt, don't criticize them in your mind. Be open and attentive—and watch the magic start to happen.

You will find yourself listening them into speech, into new ideas, into self-esteem and empowerment. You will find yourself listening both of you into the future.

Listen to Yourself, Too

And while we are so busy listening to others, we need to listen to ourselves, too.

Following Julia Cameron's suggestion in *The Artist's Way at Work*, I write three pages in my journal every morning before anyone else is up, *no matter what.* I force myself to sit down and do this. The first several years, what happened was, I found myself writing about things that worried me that weren't even on my to-do list—and were more important than the things that were. Many times what I wrote would show me ways to reframe some of the to-dos, like what if I looked at it *this* way, or what if I went to a larger context.

In the past year in my job, I have ramped up to consistently playing at the company and corporate-sector level. It all feels bigger and faster to me. Consequently, the likelihood of my getting lost or making a suboptimal move is so much greater—and it has a much greater impact. Now in my morning journal writing, I skip to the punch line and ask, Okay, Great Spirit, what do you want me to do today? Then I write three pages of whatever answers come to me.

We must listen to ourselves and to each other, and it can start small. Listening to myself by waking up at 3:00 A.M. with thoughts, fixing tea, and writing them down on paper. Reading a book and noticing our own reactions to what the author is saying. Listening to what we put down on paper. Listening to what *you* say when someone else is listening you into speech.

Radical Move

**BUILD
YOUR CADRE**

BUILD YOUR CADRE

I learned about the importance of building a cadre from Rosabeth Moss Kanter in her book *Men and Women of the Corporation.* She points out that if you are the only woman, the only person of color, the only engineer, the only one whose first language isn't English, the only one who is fat, or the only one who is *whatever* in a group, you are a token. And you will remain one unless you change that. Tokens burn out from lack of support. They can't really effect permanent change.

So the trick, if you're a token, is to become a minority, and to do it as soon as you can. One way is to aggregate—as the technical women of HP did at our conferences. As the domestic-partner proponents did by giving our Readers' Theater presentations across the company. As the deaf and hard of hearing did at their gatherings.

Employee groups like these allow tokens to quickly become minorities and then be able to change things. After all, one person can't expect the CEO to come in to talk to her about an issue. A minority group can. And often the CEO then becomes a co-conspirator.

Another beauty of building your cadre is what happens when you learn to step aside and let others lead the effort you are involved in. This not only turbocharges their energy for the project and deepens their commitment to its success, it creates another person with a desire to build *their* cadre.

Step 3: Use the Right Tool

Steps 1 and 2 lay the ground for using the tactical tools of step three.

As we go through these tools, remember that they are gardening tools. They are used to cultivate an environment where change can grow, not to force change by hammering it down. The organization is a living system, not an old Ford that needs a valve job.

SCALE UP, SCALE DOWN

This is really two tools, or one tool that works in two directions. When you come to a problem you can't figure out how to solve, or even approach, you can try scaling up or scaling down. Scaling up or down is about changing your perspective. It's about viewing a situation in different ways, the way you would see a square mile of farmland from a helicopter, an airplane, and a satellite.

Radical Tool

SCALE UP

When you scale up, you are getting above the problem, getting *bigger* than it. You have a longer view; and are automatically living on higher ground.

For example, right now we're in the start-up phase of World e-Inclusion and we're working eighteen-hour days. Scaled down to the hour-by-hour, day-in-day-out level, it's totally overwhelming. I have two hundred to-do items and about sixty are urgent. I'm churning along, adrenaline pumping, then I remember to quickly scale up, put it in perspective.

One way I'm forcing myself to scale up is every morning, no matter what, no matter if my voice mail is full with sixty messages and I'm late to a meeting, I sit down at home, put on an alto flute recording, and write in my journal. I light a stick of incense and watch the hummingbirds drink from my flowers. That's scaling up. It's locating me in the larger context of my own life, which isn't just this job.

I go off to work "up," but get scaled down by a call that my son just got kicked out of camp. So I can scale up again and say, "Well, that's bad, but seeing he's a black boy in this country, at least he wasn't shot." Then I get home and the house is a wreck and I say, "Ah, at least I have a house." I just scale, scale, scale. I can do it really fast now because it's so essential to my survival at any given point.

Jim Sheats's interest in sustainability scaled up from his evening and weekend work to the HP for Sustainability conference to his work with MIT putting cyberkiosks in villages from Latin American to Asia. The technical women at HP scaled up from tokens to a minority the moment they held their first conference. We scaled up HP Labs' Walk Through Time by inviting people from fifty nonprofits to come and take the walk. Then we scaled up the project some more by putting the exhibit on the road.

Whether we scale up by enlarging our perspective or our arena of accomplishment, we find this an infinitely valuable tool.

Scaling Down

If scaling up is getting above the problem, scaling down is getting beneath it, flying too low to be on the radar screen.

Radical Tool

SCALE DOWN

We scaled down when I was at Santa Clara Division and wanted to have a large percentage of minorities and women in our summer-intern hiring pool. At the division level, the high percentage of minorities could have caused a backlash. But when we scaled down to the level of the hiring manager, offering each manager a pool of three or four applicants, two of whom were always white males—albeit the same two!—the problem disappeared. The white kids got hired and the minorities and women got hired, too. Einstein said that you cannot solve a problem at the same level on which it was created. He is right!

Scaling down also helps us identify positive deviants, as Emily Duncan and I did at Corporate when we identified individual managers who had better minority hiring practices than the company as a whole, and then provided them visibility and resources.

AMPLIFY POSITIVE DEVIANCE

This is the most important tactical tool in this book. So if you can't deal with more than one tool, make it this one.

The principle of amplifying positive deviance is based on this simple fact: In every community in the world, certain individuals find better solutions to problems than their neighbors, despite having access to exactly the same resources.

Radical Tool

AMPLIFY
POSITIVE
DEVIANCE

These individuals are "positive deviants"— they are deviating from the norm by being more successful. Identifying these "positive deviants" can reveal hidden resources, from which it is possible to devise solutions that are cost effective, internally owned and managed, and sustainable.

"Positive deviance" contrasts sharply with traditional organization development. Positive deviance is focused on assets, not deficits. To identify a positive deviant, you have to look for what's going *right*, not what's going wrong. It puts you in a completely different frame of mind.

Positive Deviance	*Traditional Organizational Development*
• an asset model (looks for what's there, for what's right)	• a deficit model (looks for what's missing, what's wrong)
• based on indigenous wisdom that already exists within the system	• based on experts from the outside
• cheap	• expensive
• goes with flow already in the system	• disrupts the status quo
• find others in the system who are being successful • find out what they are doing differently	• find out what's wrong • try to fix it • find out what's missing • import it
• learn from them	
• stirs up relatively few antibodies because the team or organization is learning from the "next bench"	• stirs up lots of antibodies within the team or organization in reaction to experts and new ideas, processes, etc., coming from the outside
• produces change that lasts	• produces change that doesn't last

Positive deviance explains what's worked about the most dramatic changes in which I've been involved or seen up close at HP. In just about every case, people at the grassroots level who had been tooling along doing their jobs stopped and got it that the company was falling short of its promise in some dimension that they felt passionate about. Then they stepped out of their old behaviors and became positive deviants, going on to amplify their new thoughts and behaviors and so push the whole system forward.

Identify the Deviants

There are two parts to using this tool. First, you have to identify the deviants, find the people who are doing something different and better than the mainstream. You can do this by starting conversations all over the place, tapping the strengths of your relationships, or looking at the data.

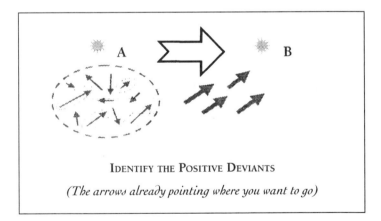

IDENTIFY THE POSITIVE DEVIANTS
(The arrows already pointing where you want to go)

When Jerry Sternin of Save the Children introduced the tool of positive deviance in Vietnamese villages where children were malnourished, he looked at the children who *weren't* starving. Their parents were clearly doing something right. They were the positive deviants in this situation. (For the complete story, read "The Power of Positive Deviancy" by Jerry Sternin and Robert Choo in the January–February 2000 issue of *Harvard Business Review*.)

Amplify Them

Once you know who your deviants are, you set to work amplifying them. You shine the light on them, get articles about them published in the company newsletter, talk them up to everyone you meet, get them together for a conference. Giving them resources—money, help, consulting—is another important way of amplifying your positive deviants.

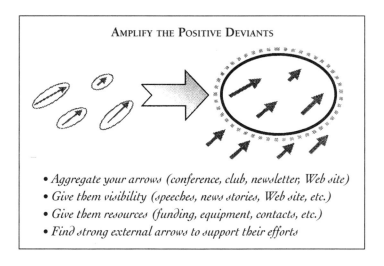

AMPLIFY THE POSITIVE DEVIANTS

- *Aggregate your arrows (conference, club, newsletter, Web site)*
- *Give them visibility (speeches, news stories, Web site, etc.)*
- *Give them resources (funding, equipment, contacts, etc.)*
- *Find strong external arrows to support their efforts*

What else can we do to exploit the potential of "positive deviance"? Here are a few ideas:

- Notice all the times it's already worked in your professional life.

- Get in touch with your wildest dreams, then frame one of them as a key part of your company's future.
- Consider yourself the positive deviant manifesting that state, right now, in the form of your dream. Now you're only a step away from reality!
- Amplify yourself by starting a conversation about your dream.
- Create a plan to scale up the conversation. Surf the company Web site and recruit kindred souls (define *kindred* very broadly and let them decide whether they're in or out; and don't worry about who's in or out—play with who shows up). Create a Web site, start a newsletter, bring in a speaker, have a conference. Invite your division, site, business and/or corporate communicator or PR rep to lunch (or even better, to the conference).

You're on your way!

Turn "Enemies" into Allies

You can think of this tool, turning your "enemies" (i.e., nonsympathizers) into allies, as a form of amplifying positive deviance. To accomplish this turnaround, find something to appreciate in the people who aren't on your wavelength. Basically, you are looking for positive deviance *within* the individual.

I spent seven years as the director of the women's center for nine theological schools in Berkeley. Using the tactics of the '60s and '70s, I did what I now see as "amplifying *negative* deviance." We caught the guys doing the worst stuff and then amplified their "crimes" through protests and writing about them. Guess what? Just like positive deviance when it's amplified, negative deviance grows and gets stronger.

Radical Tool

TURN "ENEMIES"
INTO ALLIES

In my time there, I learned the limits of using confrontation to change things, and the possibilities that opened up when I used compassion and dialogue. I saw what a tremendous loss arises from the good guys/bad guys approach: First, we miss the bad in the good guys, most importantly in ourselves; and second, we miss the good in the bad guys, which is the where the real possibility for change lies.

I told the story earlier of one of the seminary presidents whom we attacked in an effort to get better treatment of women at the theological schools: he turned and attacked back. Thankfully, he didn't succeed in disbanding our group, but it was close.

After biting and being bitten back, I began thinking about what would happen if we started finding these guys doing something right. Anything right. As it turned out, this very same guy we had trashed had an older secretary who took care of a bedridden husband and had a pretty bleak life. Every Monday morning, this seminary president would bring her fresh flowers for her desk. It was the sole point of beauty, the only bright spot in her week. We knew about this because she helped out at the center occasionally.

So, shortly after he recommended that we be disbanded, we completely shocked this man by telling him how much these flowers meant to his secretary and what a loving thing it was to do. And how grateful we were to him on her behalf that he took the time to bring this beauty into her life. That was the opening for a turnaround in our relationship with him.

Three years later, the very same man made a motion at the board of trustees meeting—where he had once advanced the idea that we be disbanded—introducing a resolution that we be commended for a decade of service.

Finding something to appreciate—and telling him—turned him from an "enemy" into an ally. A corollary to finding something "good" in the bad guys is to take something "wrong" the company is saying and consider, what if the company isn't wrong? What if there is truth when it says things?

For example, what if, when we came up with the Walk Through Time and HP said, "We're not ready to make an environmental statement," they were right? What if HP, as a company, really *wasn't* ready to make an environmental statement? Maybe we have to come up with recycling solutions for all our printer cartridges before we make a public statement.

If we can consider that the "bad" guys might be doing something that's not bad—no matter how it looks to us—we can start thinking about how to do what we want in a way that is consistent with what the company insists on. So we said to ourselves, perhaps this Walk should be not content—that is, an environmental statement—but the context for *all* our business questions and everybody else's questions at any level of scale. By allowing the company to be right for its "conservative" stance, we created a Walk with greater power, a Walk that now travels the planet.

So instead of raging that the people in power are wrong

(as we did so vociferously in the '70s), we can look for the "good" in the "bad": We can find the truth in what they are saying, respect it, and build from there.

What about a more complicated issue, like globalization? Many of us are concerned about the "bad guy" behavior of the World Trade Organization, to which many of our companies belong. It meets in private, keeps no record of its deliberations, has no appeal process, and can override local interests at every level of scale. We can respond by storming out the door of our "bad guy" corporation and joining the protesters on the street, many of whom are our friends—and some of us do.

But if we do that, we can't leverage our insider status to approach the people inside the company who are making these decisions and raise these questions as one employee to another, as one "good guy" to the good in the other guy. And we miss an enormous opportunity for the very cause for which the protesters are working. I think of this as a variation on "Turn 'enemies' into allies." I call it "See the ally in the 'enemy.'"

Many of my colleagues and I are having these conversations inside our companies and are sharing our experience, strength, progress, and hope at conferences like those held by Business for Social Responsibility and the Social Venture Network.

CHANGE THE CONTEXT OF WHAT YOU'RE DOING

Changing the ostensible purpose of the Walk Through Time by reframing it is an example of the next tool: When you run into a serious roadblock, change the context of what you are doing. You can do this by reframing the context or by going to a larger context.

Reframe the Context

There's a story about the famous seventeenth-century architect, Sir Christopher Wren, surveying the progress of the rebuilding of Saint Paul's Cathedral, which had been destroyed by the London fire of 1666. As he strolled around the building site, he came across three stonemasons. He walked up to the first one and asked the man what he was doing. "I'm cutting blocks of stone," he said testily. "Each one exactly the same as the next and the next and the next." He shook his head in disgust and went back to his task.

Radical Tool

REFRAME THE CONTEXT

Then Sir Christopher walked over to the second stonecutter and asked the man what he was doing. "I am earning my living and feeding my wife and children," he said with pride. Then he turned back to his task.

Slowly, Sir Christopher approached the third stonemason. "What are you doing, good sir?" asked the architect. The man looked up at him. His eyes were shining. "I am building a tribute to the glory of All That Is," he said with a quiet smile.

The choice of a context is ours. A sustainability conference can be something for a group of employees—or it can be a customer visit to learn what our customers need in the area of sustainability. A Walk Through Time can be an environmental message or it can be a context for asking business questions, which is, of course, what we're here to do. A conference for women employees can be about women, or it can be about contribution to the bottom line, employee retention and professional development.

Try this tool on your own conundrums. You'll see. It works.

Go to a Larger Context

In a way, this is the same thing as scaling up. The ultimate example of going to a larger context

Radical Tool

GO TO A LARGER
CONTEXT

was shifting the vision for HP Labs from being best *in* the world to being best *for* the world. The first vision got some people excited, but it wasn't bone-deep excitement because it was too small and required too little of us. The second vision, the scaled-up one, the one where we went to a *much* larger

context, got everyone excited. And we're still excited!

The largest context is always an infinite game: one whose goal is never reached, a game we lose only if we stop playing.

PLAY WITH WHOEVER SHOWS UP

When we start stirring up the silt in the interest of change, we never know who's going to come

Radical Tool

PLAY WITH
WHOEVER
SHOWS UP

to the surface. Most likely it will be the people you least expect. The ones who have been sitting in their cubicles not making waves, maybe being cynical, maybe just looking bored and boring.

Our job is to play with whoever shows up. Frankly, the people I call the alpha males and females aren't going to be the ones who show up. They are who you think you want, because they would lend status to the fledging start-up idea. But they have too much invested in the status quo and are getting too many rewards from it to want to spearhead the change.

The ones who show up are people who don't have so much invested in the way it already is, who are not lit up and getting rewarded by it. They will think out of the box and change it. They have no stake in the ground for the status quo.

A high proportion of cynics shows up—but cynics are just disappointed idealists. If you represent even a sliver of hope, some of them will come out of hiding. Often, they're brilliant.

I saw this when people started coming in to talk about their ideas for "world's best," I saw it when we put together the Celebrations of Creativity, and I continue to see it in every new apple-cart-upsetting project in which I get involved.

But the best reason that people who show up are the best ones to play with is that they're the ones who actually *show up.*

TWEAK, DON'T TOSS

A more formal name for this tool is "minimalism." It's about *not* making big changes and raising the antibody threshold. It's about making small changes that don't disrupt the system, and trusting that small changes, aggregated, result in big change.

Radical Tool

TWEAK,
DON'T TOSS

So I try to remember—not always with success—before

I go tearing in to change something, to step way back, calm down and center myself, and think about what's the least perturbation we can introduce into the system and still get the change we want. Positive deviance is a great example of "tweak, don't toss."

When you work in alignment with the principles of minimalism, you can see what else is happening besides what you *meant* to happen, and you can stop, or do something a little different, if you don't like these unintended consequences. Also, over time and with enough little efforts, a new order emerges—one that you could not have planned at an off-site, no matter how many flip charts you hauled out.

So help what wants to happen, happen. Probably just one little obstacle needs to be removed or one little ingredient added. Don't push the river. Forget the system overhaul, skip the consultants, cancel the off-sites, and give even half the money you save to employees who want to change things. Don't interrupt anyone. Let those who *want* change make it happen. Just make that 2 percent tweak.

The other reason for going slow, for tweaking instead of tossing, is based on the rules of complex living systems. One of these is called "sensitive dependence on initial conditions." It means that if you shoot a rocket to the moon and are off by a billionth of a degree at launch, by the time the rocket gets there, you'll be off by millions of miles.

So don't launch to the moon. Set your stake in the ground to reach the moon, but launch your first step. Then see what happens. Because, depending on what kind of atmosphere you are trying to get through and what kind of glitches the rocket develops, everything can change.

Do What Wants to Be Done, Do What's Doable

Here's a principle I would have sneered at in the '70s: "If it's too hard to do, it's probably not time to do it." Don't get me wrong. If it's just a lot of work and long hours, it's not "too hard." "Too hard" is when all around you, you meet resistance and negativity; no one wants to do it. There's blockage; nothing seems to be working. There's no flow.

When that happens, ask yourself, what's right in front of me to be done that *does* want to be done, that's in alignment with my vision?

When we began the program to be the "world's best," I wanted to introduce Quality tools to the R&D process, but the scientists and engineers refused. No, they said. Don't look at how we decide which technologies to work on, and how we invent and transfer. We don't want you messing with the core business. Go ahead and apply your Quality tools to Personnel, Finance, and Information Systems, but leave us alone. We're different; every invention is different. It ain't broke, so don't fix it.

So I backed off and thought maybe we should can the whole Quality idea. Then I remembered that when all else fails, do what's right in front of you. So we applied Quality tools to our personnel processes, our financial processes, our procurement, our information systems, and so on. That was what wanted to be done.

We started working on those areas and reporting the results in operations meetings. ("Here's our turnaround time on a hire and here's how much it cost and here's the benchmarking from the best companies, and we're off by orders of magnitude. We've analyzed our process and here's what we can do to change it.) Pretty soon the researchers start saying, "Don't leave us out. We want to do it too. What does this look like for the research process?" Then they start pulling stuff off the Web related to Quality tools as applied to research labs. And they start their own Quality program.

So remember, change as little as possible to get your results. This will keep you under the antibody threshold and it will still bring you success.

When you create a huge re-engineering effort that steps way back, is top-down, and is really going to be the do-all end-all, you're doomed. The inventor of "re-engineering" admits that 70 percent of these efforts fail, and he blames the failures on poor execution. Of course there is poor execution: Our organizations aren't machines that can be re-engineered! They are living systems. Any parent knows that any effort to "re-engineer" a child is futile. Any human being knows that the effort to "re-engineer" themselves is the hardest thing they ever have to do. So how on Earth is re-engineering the behavior of one hundred thousand people supposed to succeed?

You don't know what's going to happen when you start changing things in living systems. So do small. Small-scale, short-term efforts fueled by passion and commitment turn into large, long-range, and sustained transformation.

Now, it's hard to do the small stuff and only what wants to be done because all our reward and recognition systems are set up to notice the splashy, the big, the noisy stuff. Ironically, when you look back at the splashy stuff, much of it turns out to be sound and fury, signifying nothing with regard to real change. So I'm not saying you will be rewarded for starting small. But you will be *effective*. And my experience is, rewards often follow in time.

HOLD UP A MIRROR

Holding up the mirror means enabling the organization to see itself or an aspect of itself. When you get a story about your organization into the CEO's speech, that's a mirror. A Readers' Theater performance that shows management what people think is preventing HP Labs from being "best" is a mirror. This book is a mirror for HP and for HP Labs.

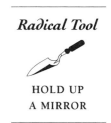

Radical Tool

HOLD UP
A MIRROR

Living systems will self-correct if they can see themselves. That's why the role of the mirror—whatever form it takes—is very powerful. When you see yourself, you can often see what to do next, things that hadn't even occurred to you.

When we used Readers' Theater to hold up the mirror on working conditions for lesbians and gay men in the company, management was dismayed: "This isn't the HP Way; we cannot have this." And suddenly the policy changed.

So hold the mirror up to see homophobia. Hold the mirror up to see racism. Hold the mirror up to see hope. Hold the mirror up to see passion. Hold the mirror up to see who cares about the four billion on this planet at the bottom of the economic pyramid.

Readers' Theater

I learned about Readers' Theater during the women's movement, where we used it as a way to raise to consciousness "taboo" issues so that people could begin to work on them—issues like sexism, racism, homophobia, and sexual abuse and harassment.

A Readers' Theater performance typically consists of two to fourteen people reading from a notebook their own or other folks' stories about a certain topic or issue. A script usually lasts about half an hour. The people whose stories are told can remain anonymous, and the readers do not necessarily read their own stories.

As you have read in this memoir, I have used Readers' Theater many times at HP, and each time it has had a significant impact. For a complete rundown of how to do Readers' Theater and some examples of scripts, go to:

www.hpl.hp.com/hosted/wbirl/readers/

That's my tool kit. Please borrow from it, steal from it, and add to it. As you engage in your own corporate revolution, you will find that the ideas for tools come from doing the work. They also come from our spiritual co-conspirators—those around us and those in books. Following the Index is a list of books that matter to me. And a little music, too!

APPENDICES

HOW COULD MY EXPERIENCE BE MORE USEFUL TO YOU?

There are many ways to tell a story, many places from which to tell it.

Let me know how talking about my journey could be more useful to you in your own. I'll incorporate what I can in the next edition, or the next book.

Let me know what would help: I promise to listen. Here are the questions that prompted three complete versions of this manuscript before it was even published. I hope they prompt a response from you.

1. What works?
2. What do these memoirs allow for, for you at the personal level, and the organizational, community, and global levels?
3. What doesn't work?
4. What's missing?

Send me your comments at:

barbarawaugh100@hotmail.com

SHARE YOUR STORY FOR THE NEXT BOOK

how have you fomented revolution, large or small, where you work?

Tell me about it. Tell me who you are, what the problem was that you wanted to solve, how and when you did it, and who helped you. Tell me how your effort worked out. And include your name, telephone, and e-mail address so I can contact you when I write volume two, consisting of your stories.

My goal is to put together a book telling the stories of corporate revolutionaries around the globe who are asking more of themselves and each other.

Please note: If you don't want your story or your name used in such a book, say so at the top of your story. Otherwise I'll assume you're ready to go public with your revolutionary acts!

Send me your stories at:

barbarawaugh100@hotmail.com

ACKNOWLEDGMENTS

I offer my *deep gratitude to the people who have guided and* partnered with me on this journey.

FOR INSPIRING ME TO PLAY AT THE WORLD-LEVEL OF SCALE AND SHOW-
ING US ALL HOW:

Muhammad Yunus for the dream, the plan, and the path to put material poverty into the museum of history, and for making me and my company partners in the dream; Alex Counts for keeping the dream and the relationship alive for years in the face of little hope; Bill Strickland for the dream, the plan, and the path to turn inner cities into places of light and hope, and for making me and my company partners in the dream;

FOR INSPIRATION, SUPPORT, AND PARTNERSHIP FOR CORPORATE REVOLU-
TION AT HP, INCLUDING ALL MY BEST "FOR THE WORLD" BUDDIES AT HP
LABS:

Carly Fiorina for transforming "radical" from a career-limiting epithet to HP's highest compliment, and for opening the garage to every employee and for the world; Lew Platt for support and listening that extends to this day; Joel Birnbaum for cosmic technology visions that could enable the world to work for everyone, and for always believing in a bigger *me* than I do and lending me strength to grow; Debra Dunn for ongoing reality checks that enable a wild new vision to take root and grow; Ed Karrer and Dick Lampman for the kind of leading from above that inspires, evokes, and supports leading from below;

Emily Duncan for strategies to make diversity hiring and domestic-partner benefits a reality; Barb Recchia, the Barb that made it to the front page of the *New York Times*; Laurie Mittelstadt for shoulder-to-shoulder partnership that makes anything possible and most of it fun; Hazen Witemeyer for brilliance, youth, and the willingness and courage to grow; Andrew Liu for being a best friend at my worst times and modeling the courage to stop when it's time; Sharon Connor for your gentle and firmly principled can-do approach to everything you do; Cheryl Ritchie and Bob Waites for modeling loyalty to excellence and truth above personality and politics;

Cheryl Ritchie, Jay Coleman, Shirley Gilbert, and Glenda Dasmalchi for defining "open" communication as truth, courage, and partnership; Srinivas Sukumar and Susan Burnett for leadership from the side on reframing out-of-the-box ideas so they get in under the antibody threshold; Ian Osborne for partnership in the early WBIRL years and friendship ever since; Vivian Wright for going to where it all breaks down and sharing the gifts of that place; John Wilkes for Victorian woodcuts in technical talks, weekends on the surveys, wry humor, and ongoing support; Bill Worley for exploring beyond what we know and comparing findings with me; Rosanne Wyleczuk for "getting" and leapfrogging every idea from Grameen to global education; Catherine Slater for courage under fire, "fat sheep," and brilliant insights about life and change; Betty Sproule for "Wise Ornery Women," inspiration, and counsel; Jean Tully for knowing everybody and doing whatever it takes to connect us; Ron Crough for original, pragmatic, clear distinctions and change strategies; Denny Georg for making me your coach and becoming mine; Marvin Keshner for sharing with me all you are—Native American and African drummer, tent builder, technologist, and friend; Karn MacGregor for courage on the uphill climbs and persistence with the details of my ongoing life; Simone Frost for brilliant fixes and great strategy with the equipment in my life; Neerja Raman for consistent partnership and quiet courage with technology and innovation for the dream; Eugenie Prime for "astonishing ourselves" with our dreams and projects; Cathy Lipe for inspired response and constant partnership as we strategize HP's transformation on behalf of the poor; John Hassell for spirited response, "being and becoming beloved," and co-invention going forward; Deborah Hudson for spirited reading, two articles, and "harleys to the crone"; and all my other "Best in and for the World" buddies at HP Labs, for provoking me into thought, hearing me into speech, and appreciating me into relevance;

FOR PARTNERSHIP WITH, INSPIRATION FOR, AND IDEAS ABOUT HOW TO CHANGE THE WORLD, MY CIRCLE OF CONSULTANT AND ARTIST FRIENDS:

Ed Gurowitz, Mel Toomey, and Joyce Dowdall for generative thinking and distinctions that allow for "transferring technology"; Dana Toomey for celebrating spirit in word, metal, and stone; Kristin Cobble for being the first, and for hearing me into distinctions and the chapter; Rayona Sharpnack for making the complex simple so we get the possibilities of our lives, and for amplifying me into a star; John O'Neil for sharing your thoughts and valuing my judgments; Warren Bennis for gracious, generous encouragement and eldering; Juanita Brown for sharing all you have, from your path so like mine, to your home, to "community organizing," to all you know; Meg Wheatley for passion, courage, and persistence for the dream.

MY WORLD E-INCLUSION BUDDIES AT AND BEYOND HP:

Jim Sheats for being the first, being original, and insisting on the possibilities; Lyle Hurst for the business-focused dream that the world's rural poor enjoy Internet-enabled benefits "in my language, in my village, appropriate to my culture"; Therese Tong for being the first hire and for for-the-world dreams for laughter and keeping on; Hafsat Abiola for combining so utterly the extremes of wisdom and youth, compassion and fire, and for partnership going forward; Jim Moore for passion, brilliance, boldness, and partnership in the World e-Inclusion dream; Bob Saldich for humor, perspective, and co-mentoring; Anne Firth Murray for a new paradigm of philanthropy—the venture capitalists and the entrepreneurs in global sisterhood on behalf of women's human rights; Diane Mailey and Lynne Twist for grace, courage, and inspiration under fire, again and again; Susan Davis for soul-sister-hood, dreaming and incarnating miracles from Wall Street to Nigeria, lifetime after lifetime;

FOR THE FRIENDS WHO PUT AND KEEP ME IN FAST COMPANY:

John Seely Brown for listening me into stories of my latest projects and then siccing *Fast Company* magazine onto me; Alan Webber, Bill Taylor, and Katharine Mieszkowski for putting and keeping me in *Fast Company*; Alan Webber for partnering as a soul brother in the bigger dream that gives rise to our projects; Chip Conley for *The Rebel Rules*, joie de vivre, and being my kid brother; Chris Turner for *All Hat—* and all the cattle too (sister activist inside); Mark Albion for listening me into writing my own book and, until I did, including me in all of yours; Harriet Rubin for envisioning multiple futures for this book not even written, and thus conjuring it;

FOR PARTNERSHIP IN MAKING THIS BOOK:

Lisa Lion Wolfe and Catherine Slater for enthusiastically reading me into the first drafts; Tyler Norris and the Kellogg Fellows, 1999, for listening me into the five-minute version of this story, thereby giving me the outline for this book; Richard Pascale for stellar walks, soul talks, and partnership in the dream that this story be told; Margot Silk Forrest, my coauthor, for "putting together the puzzle pieces" of tapes, talks, interviews, and me, giving me my best hour of each of twelve weeks, this story, and this book, all three versions, and always taking the highest road whenever faced with a choice; Rhonda Kirk for wonderful art on the early covers of this book; Marc Schuyler for vetting the HP story "for the world"; Lisa Carr and Susan Schettino for enthusiastic support and specific suggestions on closer ties to HP's Reinvention and the Rules of the Garage; John Elder, Chip McClelland, and John Nelson at Inner Ocean Publishing for enthusiastic embrace of the manuscript; Bill Greaves for a cover that uplifts the whole message; Beth Hansen-Winter for her exquisite interior design; our editor, Roger Jellinek, for gentle prodding and subtle hints that inspired Margot and me to make a better book; Barbara Drew for her stylistic upgrade; and our agent, Amy Rennert, who acted with intelligence and persistence in our behalf;

FOR MY BIRTH AND EXTENDED FAMILY:

My parents, Capt. James C. Waugh and Maxine Procter Waugh, for the curiosity and courage to seek ever larger worlds; my brother, Jim Waugh, sister-in-law Peggy Blake, and my sisters, Meg Koc and Betsy Toro, for cheering me on; our "village"—Michael Kass, Scott Bowers, Carol Miller, Janina Nadaner, Carol Beaumont, Ellen Stabinsky, and Carol Zepecki—for making our kids' schools "for the world," a tougher challenge than a corporation;

Al Moye ("Daddy Al"), Jim Koch, Emily Duncan ("Aunt Em") and Joe Tibbs ("Uncle Joe"), Bess Stephens, and Eugenie Prime for all the lunches, calls, and keeping connected, and for your courage to live the possibility of a corporation where talent is valued and promoted regardless of race and a family that extends beyond blood; Jay Davidson for salty, bracing walks and talks; Peppermint for keeping the cave in enough order to remain charmingly livable; Anastasia Cusulos, my life's partner for twenty-five years of co-creating all that matters;

And Alexis and Jordan, our children, for the inspiration and necessity to keep going.

Parts of these memoirs have appeared or been heard elsewhere. Heartfelt thanks to each of these venues for "hearing me into speech."

INSIDE HP

- 1993 Technical Women's Conference, "Beads on a String"
- 1995 Technical Women's Conference, "Diversity Journeys"
- 1995 Technical Women's Conference, "Change Managers' Readers' Theater"
- 1995 Deaf and Hard of Hearing Forum Keynote
- 1996 Regional Women's Conference, "Quest vs. Quilt"
- 1998 Regional Women's Conference, "Discovering Your Unique Contributions"
- 2000 Radical Thoughts, HPnow company newsletter, "Positive Deviance"
- Hewlett Packard Company Web Pages:

www.hpl.hp.com/hosted/wbirl
<http://www.hpl.hp.com/hosted/wbirl>

www.hpl.hp.com/hosted/wbirl/readers/
<http://www.hpl.hp.com/hosted/wbirl/readers/>

www.hp.com/e-inclusion
<http://www.hp.com/e-inclusion>

OUTSIDE HP

- Conley, Chip. *The Rebel Rules: Daring to Be Yourself in Business*. Simon & Schuster, 2001.
- Leonard, Dorothy, and Walter Swap. *When Sparks Fly: Igniting Creativity in Groups*. Harvard Business School Press, 1999.

- McMeekin, Gail. *The 12 Secrets of Highly Creative Women: A Portable Mentor*. Conari Press, 2000.
- Pascale, Richard, Mark Millemann, and Linda Gioja. *Surfing the Edge of Chaos: The Laws of Nature and the New Laws of Business*. Crown Business, 2000.
- Senge, Peter, Art Kleiner, Charlotte Roberts, George Roth, and Bryan Smith. *The Dance of Change*. Doubleday, 1999, 507-509.
- *Fast Company*, December 1998, "Who's Fast 1999," 146-57.
- *Fast Company*, February 2000, "Take the Brand Challenge"
- *Fast Company*, March 2000, "Fast Pack 2000," 234-54.
- Systems Thinking in Action Conference, 1997
- Linkage Leadership Conferences, 1998, 1999
- Business and Professional Women's Conferences, 1998, 1999, 2000
- Fast Company Realtime, Naples, Florida, 1998
- Fast Company Advance, Nantucket, 1999
- Strategos Revolutionaries Conference, 2000
- Fast Company Realtime, Phoenix, 2000

Margot Silk Forrest
707 Buena Vista Ave., Moss Beach, CA 94038
tel. 650/728-7058   fax 650/728-1324

margotsf@mindspring.com

**www.margotsilkforrest.com <http://
www.margotsilkforrest.com/>**

INDEX

BOOKS THAT MATTER

Albion, Mark S. *Making a Life, Making a Living*. Warner, 2000.

Aristide, Jean Bertrand. *Eyes of the Heart*. Common Courage Press, 2000.

Bateson, Mary Catherine. *Composing a Life*. Plume, 1990.

Bennis, Warren. *An Invented Life: Reflections on Leadership and Change*. Addison Wesley Longman, 1993.

Bennis, Warren. *Managing the Dream*. Perseus, 2000.

Bornstein, David. *The Price of a Dream: The Story of Grameen Bank*. University of Chicago Press, 1997.

Bryan, Mark, with Julia Cameron and Catherine Allen. *The Artist's Way at Work*. William Morrow, 1998.

Cameron, Julia, *The Right to Write*. J.P. Tarcher, 1999.

Carse, James. *Finite and Infinite Games*. Ballantine, 1986.

Christensen, Clayton. *Innovator's Dilemma*. Harvard Business School Press, 1997.

Collins, James C., and Jerry I. Porras. *Built to Last*. HarperCollins, 1994.

Conley, Chip. *The Rebel Rules: Daring to Be Yourself in Business*. Simon & Schuster, 2001.

Counts, Alex. *Give Us Credit*. Times Books/Random House, 1996. This book is out of print but is available through the Grameen Foundation, USA. To order, contact them at (202) 628-3560 or *www.grameenfoundation.org*.

Eisenhardt, Kathy. *Competing on the Edge*. Harvard Business School Press, 1998.

Gladwell, Malcolm. *The Tipping Point*. Little, Brown, 2000.

Godin, Seth. *Unleashing the Ideavirus*. Do You Zoom, 2000.

Goldberg, Natalie. *Writing Down the Bones*. Shambala, 1986.

Hamel, Gary. *Leading the Revolution*. Harvard Business School Press, 2000.

Harrison, Roger. *The Consultant's Journey*. Jossey-Bass, 1995.

Jaworski, Joseph. *Synchronicity*. Berrett-Koehler Publishers, 1996.

Kanter, Rosabeth Moss. *Men and Women of the Corporation*. Basic Books, 1977.

Kelly, Kevin. *Out of Control: The New Biology of Machines, Social Systems and the Economic World*. Addison Wesley, 1994.

Kirk-Duggan, Cheryl A. *Exorcizing Evil*. Orbis Books, 1997.

Kleiner, Art. *The Age of Heretics*. Doubleday, 1996.

Komisar, Randy. *The Monk and the Riddle*. Harvard Business School Press, 2000.

Lawrence-Lightfoot, Sara. *I've Known Rivers*. Penguin Books, 1994.

Liebes, Sid, Elisabet Sahtoris, and Brian Swimme. *A Walk Through Time: From Stardust to Us*. John Wiley & Sons, 1998.

McMeekin, Gail. *The 12 Secrets of Highly Creative Women: A Portable Mentor*. Conari Press, 2000.

Moore, Geoffrey. *Crossing the Chasm*. HarperBusiness, 1991.

Morton, Nelle. *The Journey Is Home*. Beacon Press, 1985.

Muller, Wayne. *Sabbath: Restoring the Sacred Rhythm of Rest*. Bantam Doubleday Dell, 1999.

O'Neil, John. *Leadership Aikido: Six Business Practices That Can Turn Your Life Around*. Three Rivers Press, 1999.

———. *The Paradox of Success: When Winning at Work Means Losing at Life*. J.P. Tarcher, 1994.

Owen, Harrison. *Expanding Our Now: The Story of Open Space Technology*. Berrett-Koehler, 1997.

———. *Leadership Is*. Berrett-Koehler, 1997.

———. *Open Space Technology: A User's Guide*. Berrett-Koehler, 1997.

Packard, David. *The HP Way: How Bill Hewlett and I Built Our Company*. HarperCollins, 1995.

Pascale, Richard, Mark Millemann, and Linda Gioja. *Surfing the Edge of Chaos: The Laws of Nature and the New Laws of Business*. Crown Business, 2000.

Rubin, Harriet. *The Princessa: Machiavelli for Women*. Bantam Double-day Dell, 1997.

Rubin, Harriet. *Soloing: Realizing Your Life's Ambition*. HarperCollins, 1999.

Sen, Amartya. *Development As Freedom*. Anchor Books, 2000.

Senge, Peter, Art Kleiner, Charlotte Roberts, George Roth, and Bryan Smith. *The Dance of Change*. Doubleday, 1999.

Some, Sobunfu. *The Spirit of Intimacy: Ancient African Teachings in the Ways of Relationships*. Quill, 2000.

———. *Welcoming Spirit Home: Ancient African Teachings to Celebrate Children and Community*. New World Library, 1999.

Sternin, Jerry, and Robert Choo. "The Power of Positive Deviancy." *Harvard Business Review*, January–February 2000.

Turner, Chris. *All Hat and No Cattle: Tales of a Corporate Outlaw*. Perseus, 1999.

Webber, Alan M., and William C. Taylor. *Going Global: Four Entrepreneurs Map the New World Marketplace*. Viking, 1996.

Weisman, Alan. *Gaviotas*. Chelsea Green, 1999.

Wheatley, Meg. *Leadership and the New Science*. Berrett-Koehler, 1992.

Yunus, Muhammad. *Banker to the Poor: Micro-Lending and the Battle Against World Poverty*, 2d ed. Public Affairs, 1999. (Currently out of print.)

Magazine

Webber, Alan M., and William C. Taylor, founding editors. *Fast Company*, 1997–present.

Music

Jaeger, Rolf. *Eternal Voyage*. Pacific Sound, 1998.

———. *Music from Mind and Soul*. Pacific Sound, 1991.

———. *Sonic Metamorphosis*. Pacific Sound, 1995. (*Rolf Jaeger's CDs are available through his Web site: www.california.com/—rolfj/*)

ABOUT THE AUTHORS

*B*ARBARA WAUGH *is co-founder of HP's World e-Inclusion, a* business whose goal is to provide the four billion people at the bottom of the world's economic pyramid with access to the benefits of the Internet and the new economy.

She has worked for change, one way or another, during her entire seventeen years at HP: as Santa Clara Division's staffing manager, as HP's corporate recruiting manager, as HP Labs' personnel manager, as the director of HP Labs' program to become the "Best in and for the World," and as HP Labs' worldwide change manager. Now she is a member of the World e-Inclusion team, developing profitable and sustainable business models for doing well by doing good.

She has also worked as a car mechanic, machinist, actress, journalist, teacher, therapist, social activist, and community organizer, and draws on her experience in these roles to craft change in HP. She was on the board of directors of the Pacific Cultural Conservancy International (1998–99) on the board of the State of the World Forum (1997–99), and, as of this writing, is on the board of advisors for the Global Fund for Women.

She has an M.A. in German from Florida State University, an M.A. in theology and comparative literature from the University of Chicago, and a Ph.D. in psychology and organizational behavior from the Wright Institute in Berkeley, California.

She lives in Silicon Valley with her partner, Stacy Cusulos, and their two children, Alexis and Jordan. Barb can be reached at

barbarawaugh100@hotmail.com

She is donating her earnings from the sale of this book to nonprofit organizations that support "for the world" efforts.

◆ ◆ ◆

*M*ARGOT SILK FORREST *is a writer, freelance book editor,* and the co-author of *EMDR: The Breakthrough Therapy for Trauma*. A former newspaper editor, technical writer, and top-ranked manager at Hewlett-Packard, the thing she is most proud of in her life is starting The Healing Woman Foundation (1992–2000), an international organization to support women in recovery from sexual abuse.

Margot is currently writing *The Ten Laws of the Universe, According to Me*, an eccentric and heartfelt book about the importance of love and the relative unim-portance of everything else.

She lives near San Francisco and can be reached via her Web site:

www.MargotSilkForrest.com.

A portion of her earnings from this book will go to support her new Web site for survivors of childhood sexual abuse,

www.ForYourHealing.com.

RECORD YOUR COMMENTS!

*P*ass on The Soul in the Computer *to a friend, along with* your experience of it: comments, questions, dreams with which you got in touch. Guaranteed: You'll have a great conversation with the friend you give it to!